CREATING THE PERFECT DESIGN BRIEF

second edition

HOW TO MANAGE DESIGN FOR STRATEGIC ADVANTAGE

PETER L. PHILLIPS

ALLWORTH PRESS
NEW YORK

dmi
Design Management Institute

Allworth Press books may be purchased in bulk at special discounts for sales promotion, corporate gifts, fund-raising, or educational purposes. Special editions can also be created to specifications. For details, contact the Special Sales Department, Allworth Press, 307 West 36th Street, 11th Floor, New York, NY 10018 or info@skyhorsepublishing.com

15 14 13 12 11   5 4 3 2 1

Published by Allworth Press, an imprint of Skyhorse Publishing, Inc.
307 West 36th Street, 11th Floor, New York, NY 10018.

Allworth Press® is a registered trademark of Skyhorse Publishing, Inc.®, a Delaware corporation.
www.allworth.com

Cover design by Danielle Ceccolini

Library of Congress Cataloging-in-Publication Data is available on file.
ISBN: 978-1-58115-914-1

Printed in the United States of America

This book is dedicated to
Benjamin J. Phillips
and Rebecca L. Phillips.

Contents

Chapter 15

Preface to the Second Edition

When I wrote the first edition of this book, I had no idea of how enormous the worldwide interest would be in the topic of design briefs.

The first edition has been translated into Spanish, Portuguese, and Estonian. I have been asked to address the topic at design conferences, seminars, and workshops in Asia, Europe, South America, and all over North America. The many reviews have been very positive, and I am flattered that a number of design schools, colleges, and universities worldwide have been using the book as a supplemental textbook for design students.

Throughout all of my seminars and workshops I have learned that the topic of design briefs is still not very well understood or utilized properly in the majority of enterprises I have partnered with. Many companies have adopted my system, and nearly all of them have reported great success in using my techniques.

I also learned that one very critical topic was not mentioned in my book. That topic is the increasing importance of intellectual property law to designers globally.

For this updated second edition, I collaborated with Joshua L. Cohen, a shareholder in the intellectual property rights law firm of RatnerPrestia. I first met Josh at a design conference a few years ago, and was very impressed at his ability to translate what is sometimes complex legal language into something that was easy for designers like me to grasp.

I was also fortunate to meet Soren Peterson, PhD. Dr. Peterson has been working with people at the Stanford University Center for Design Research for the past several years. His particular research interest has been the utilization of design briefs as a tool for innovation in industrial design.

Dr. Peterson's quantitative findings have served to reinforce my own qualitative experience as a practicing design manager.

Not long ago, I was chatting with an old friend and colleague in the design profession. We were talking about the dramatic changes in the design profession over the last twenty years. These changes are a result of new technology, a more intensely competitive marketplace, economic conditions, and new business models and practices.

However, with all the changes in the design profession, modern design brief practices have remained somewhat a mystery to both commissioners of design projects and designers. The most common excuse (backed up by Soren Peterson's research) is that taking the time to develop a comprehensive design brief is too time consuming, too costly, and "not our traditional approach."

All of these excuses are invalid. The world is more complicated today, and the need for developing good design briefs is more critical than ever before.

I hope that this second edition of the book will set you on the correct path if you are not accustomed to developing design briefs.

Peter L. Phillips

Acknowledgments

Not too long ago, while on a business trip, I was in my hotel room one evening watching television. A game show was on and the host had just begun the process of introducing the contestants. One contestant identified himself as a graphic designer. With an innocence I found startling, the host asked, "Does that require any kind of formal training?"

In spite of what a number of people apparently think, design professionals are trained, mentored, encouraged, and developed by a large group of people throughout their lives. We are not just "born" designers. Certainly my life and career have been particularly rich with such people. I could never have attempted to write this book thirty years ago. I just didn't have the experience or technical knowledge to attempt such an endeavor. Recently, someone asked me how long it took to write this book. It's an old cliché, but the real answer is, "About forty-five years!" It is important to me to give credit to those people who have encouraged, trained, and mentored me over the decades.

I believe the most important people were my parents, who recognized very early that I had a strong aptitude for the arts. They enrolled me in an art school when I was only ten years old. Mrs. Brown, my teacher, was the first to help me realize that "art" was much more than drawing well. I will be forever indebted to the late Mrs. Brown for her patience and encouragement at such an early age.

Later, I had the privilege of studying design with people such as Paul Zalanski, Jerry Rojo, Bob Corrigan, Don Murry, and Professor Frank Ballard, a man who taught me more about design and life in the design profession than any other person I have ever known.

More recently, I have connected with Josh Cohen, an intellectual property rights attorney, and Dr. Soren Peterson, who has been heavily engaged in global research concerning the utilization of design briefs in industrial design projects. I am indebted to both of these people for their support of my work.

In the corporate world, I was fortunate to have many mentors who were nondesigners but who helped me understand the role of design in business. These people include Art Kiernan, Peter Jancourtz, John Dickman, John Babington, Dick Berube, John Sims, David Truslow, Mike Maginn, Bob Lee, Robin Aslin, James Manderson, Hein Becht, Paul Jaeger, Dick Pienkos, D.W. Johnson, Jim Speedlin, Coleman Mockler, Karl Speak, and especially Professor Stephen A. Greyser of the Harvard Business School, a collaborator, mentor, teacher, and friend.

Over the years, I have also had the privilege of knowing and collaborating with a very large number of design management professionals. Through discussion and often heated debate, these people have helped me clarify my thinking about design and the management of design. There are so many that it would be folly to try to list and thank them all, but a few are particularly critical to acknowledge here: Wally Olins, Tony Key, Jeremy Rewes-Davies, Rodney Fitch, Rick Marciniak, Peter Fallon, Fred Martins, Jim Aggazi, Yolanda Launder, Bonnie Briggs, Jon Craine, Steven Conlon, Bill Hannon, Roz Goldfarb, Fennemiek Gommer, Peter Gorb, James Hansen, Mark Oldach, Tony Parisi, John Tyson, Raymond Turner, Peter Trussler, Gary vanDeursen, and Earl Powell, former president of the Design Management Institute.

There are so many more, but space does not permit me to list another hundred or so names! I am also grateful to all the participants who have attended my seminars and lectures. I always learn from these students.

Finally, I would like to thank my children, Benjamin and Rebecca, who have had to put up with my often hectic schedules and deadlines but always understood and maintained their belief in what I have been trying to do as a design professional.

Introduction

When I went to college to study design in the Sixties, the subject of design briefs was never mentioned. Fortunately, today the topic is finding its way into design curriculums, albeit slowly.

In college, our instructors gave us specific assignments every week. These were well-crafted design problems to solve; I suppose one could argue these were a form of design brief. However, these assignments were never called "design briefs" per se.

When I entered the corporate world a few years later as manager of a small design group, I learned very quickly that marketing people indeed prepared design briefs and handed them to the design group. We were expected to follow their briefs without much question or discussion. More often than not, these briefs frustrated me and my group of designers. These briefs rarely contained the type of information we really needed in order to create an effective design solution. Furthermore, the deadlines we were given were always impossibly short. To make matters worse, we rarely had the opportunity to have any kind of meaningful dialogue with the individual who had written the brief in the first place. Instead, a direct report of that individual, often called a "project manager," was assigned to monitor our progress. These project managers rarely were able to supply the information we so desperately wanted and needed.

I looked for some written body of knowledge on the subject and came up more or less empty. There were some articles in various design magazines that touched on design briefs, or "creative briefs," but I could not find any definitive books on the subject. Today, some forty years later, to the best of my knowledge, there are still no books available about design briefs, except for this one, and the subject is only vaguely covered in many notable professional design curriculums.

However, the practice of using some kind of brief in the design process prevails in the corporate world, forcing many of us in the design profession to try to figure out how to deal with these things in some kind of meaningful way.

Several years ago, the Design Management Institute (DMI) developed the Professional Development Program to offer design professionals an opportunity to enhance their managerial skills in a variety of areas. A survey was conducted asking DMI members what topics they would most like to see included in this new program. The design brief was in the top ten. I was asked to create a professional development seminar on the topic. Since the publication of the first edition of this book, I have also done a great many workshops for in-house groups independently, and lectured on the topic for a number of design associations worldwide.

Utilizing my own experience with design briefs and the design brief process, as well as the collective experience of a number of other professional design managers, I created a seminar that has now been attended by designers and design managers from around the globe. The response has been extremely positive to this particular seminar. As a result of this success and the additional insights I have gathered from all the seminar participants about design briefs commonly in use today, I was asked to write this book.

No Magic Formulas

It is important to understand there is no magic formula here. If there were just one correct format to use in creating the perfect design brief, all of our lives would be far less complicated! So please don't look for a single one-size-fits-all perfect design brief format here. It doesn't exist. Rather, this book covers the key ingredients that any good design brief should contain, and the critical processes (including changing the way designers *think* about design briefs) involved in creating a design brief that is truly useful to *all* individuals involved with a design project. The best design brief process is a business-oriented, strategic process; therefore this book also describes the various ways the design profession must rethink management of design as a strategic process.

It is also important to remember that there are a variety of design disciplines, and each discipline requires slightly different information in a truly useful design brief. A brief for a print project such as a brochure or catalog would probably not require any engineering elements. However, an industrial design brief for the design of a new product or tool would most likely contain information related to engineering and manufacture. A design brief for a packaging project would likewise need to contain information specifically related to package design, as well as package engineering.

During the past few years, I have also come to grips with the fact that the concept of the term *design* has changed dramatically. I have a designer friend who has a hobby of photographing signage using the term *design* during his travels worldwide. He has shown me his slide show with businesses that state they are: Pizza Designers, Dog Designers, Fingernail Designers, Insurance Coverage Designers, and Employee Health Benefit Package Designers. The term seems to be used by everybody and anybody.

Please understand this book is intended primarily for people involved with graphic design, packaging design, and industrial design projects. It won't be of much help if you design pizzas.

Readers must understand that the process is complicated by these differences, as well as by the differences in the way various enterprises structure their design resources. Therefore, it is necessary for each design organization to create its own specific set of standards, processes, and guidelines for its design briefs. This book is intended to help design professionals create those processes and formats effectively and efficiently.

Chapter 1
What Is a Design Brief Anyway?

During the course of teaching my seminar, *Creating the Perfect Design Brief,* I have learned that people use a variety of terms for what I am calling a *design brief.* Many people refer to them as a *creative brief.* Others are accustomed to other terms such as *marketing brief, project brief, job ticket,* or *innovation brief.* Whatever the term used, we are talking about a written description of a project that requires some form of visual design.

My least favorite term is *job ticket.* This is usually no more than a one-page summary of the title of the project, the due date, the budget, the name of the requesting person or group, and other mostly tactical data such as quantities, shipping instructions, and so on. In my opinion, most of these job tickets are more or less useless for the actual process of developing a design solution.

I am, on the other hand, quite taken with *innovation brief,* a term commonly used in Europe. I like what that implies.

Unfortunately, most businesses don't regard design as an innovative, or even a strategic business process. Rather, they think of it as a decorative service.

The Format of a Design Brief

Actually, there is no single correct or preferred format for a design brief. I have seen really good design briefs that are totally narrative, written in paragraph form, and others that employ the bulleted list format. Increasingly, I am seeing design briefs that have been developed with a computer program format wherein requestors for design work simply fill in the blanks after a list of key questions. I have also seen some excellent briefs formatted as PowerPoint presentations.

The format you will eventually adopt will depend largely on the specific type of design work you are involved with (industrial, graphic, packaging, etc.), and the most useful style for your company. The format is, of course, critical in that it should be easy to read and track through. Other than that, what is most important is that the brief contains *all* of the information and data necessary for every stakeholder in the process. It must also be available in hard copy, as well as online.

The computer-generated type of format seems to offer the biggest challenges to designers I have talked with over the years. It is ironic that for the most part, designers have developed these computer-generated formats! It's not so much that the formats are poorly designed, but rather that the design brief format is not used properly. The most common complaint is that many fields are left blank by the requestor(s), or if they are filled in, the information is incomplete. A typical example is a field that would be headlined, "Audience." A typical answer in this field is, "Customers." For me, that's not a suitable entry!

Finding the best format for your organization should not be overlooked. It will take some time, and experimentation, to develop a format that will meet the real-world needs of everyone in your company. I will admit, I have always found that the narrative format has worked best for me. My second choice would be the bulleted list approach.

How Long Should a Design Brief Be?

The quick answer to "How long should a design brief be?" is, "As long as necessary." A great many participants in my design brief seminar tell me they have been asked repeatedly to make design briefs as *short* as possible. That should not be the goal. The real goal is to make design briefs as *complete* and *useful* as possible. The final length will ultimately be determined by the requirements of the specific project and its complexity.

Stir-Frying a Creative Concept

Kim Zarney, president and creative director of Zarney Creative, a package design firm, wrote an article for DMI's *Design Management Journal*[1] entitled, "The Core Creative Concept in Branding: A Streamlined Approach." I particularly appreciated Kim's analogy comparing design briefs to stir-fry cooking. In fact, I have used this article as a jumping-off point for discussion in many of my design brief seminars. I also appreciate the fact that Mr. Zarney advocates a comprehensive design brief as the starting point for discovering "core creative concepts." I have received permission to include a portion of his article in this book. There are two reasons I wanted to include his article: 1) It's a powerful testimonial from one design practitioner on the benefits of developing a comprehensive design brief *prior* to beginning the process of developing creative concepts, and 2) the article makes it very clear that spending the time to develop a design brief is critical.

Excerpt from Design Management Journal, *by Kim Zarney*

The Core Creative Concept in Branding: A Streamlined Approach

Anyone who enjoys stir-fry cooking knows the key to a delicious meal is having all your ingredients ready before you get started. Stir-frying is a rapid process and it works best when you add each ingredient at just the right time. It's a fun and easy way to cook—if you are prepared.

Implementing a successful packaging program in today's business environment is a lot like stir-fry cooking. There's a sense of urgency; everything is a priority, it seems, and it all has to be done at the same time. As designers, our responsibility to help clients achieve bottom-line results is constantly challenged by limited budgets, inflexible retail merchandising requirements, tight production schedules, and shrinking delivery times. The pressure is on to make sure packaging solutions will work. At the same time, with more product choices and increasing quantities of visual clutter all competing for the consumer's attention, it's more important than ever to simplify branding messages.

The best way to achieve all these goals is to have a core creative concept to drive all the branding elements needed for a launch. Think of it as a recipe for fast-tracking the entire process. In order to establish a clear, simple message in the minds of consumers, we first need a clear understanding of what this concept needs to communicate. The more specific the message, the more effective it can be in generating the results we want.

Print advertising has always understood how this creative formula works. The timeless appeal of a great ad is its ability to tell a story, without the need for a lot of extra words or explanation. The visual impact pulls us in, and the intellectual delight keeps us there. Even though packaging is physically more complex than the printed page, the opportunity is still there to tell a simple story and make an emotional connection with the target audience.

The Ingredients

To create that special meal, you need to find the right recipe—one that outlines all the ingredients, instructions, and special techniques you're going to need. The same rationale is true for developing a core creative concept to help guide your new packaging program. The process starts with a review of your design and marketing brief to determine what you actually have to work with. It's the only place that lists all the key ingredients of the "what" of your message; analyzing those ingredients, and combining them with your own marketplace observations, will eventually help determine the "how." The end result of this front-end review and analysis should be a written brief that links the creative objectives with the business objectives. It will serve as a benchmark to test your concept as you move through the process.

The benefits of putting your brief in writing rather than just "talking it through" will become abundantly clear once your program gets underway. Everyone needs to be in sync and have the same information as things heat up. Remember, it's all about speed. Getting products to market faster, connecting with consumers quicker, and moving off the shelf faster gets the bottom-line results everyone wants.

The Inflexible Elements

Building a core creative concept should always start with a review of all the inflexible elements—the parameters within which you must work. First on the list is finding out how much time you have; that way, you'll know how much "wiggle room" you have to explore alternative solutions. For instance, your product launch may require multiple packaging formats, which will mean multiple vendor sources—and vendor deadlines usually aren't coordinated to maximize your time or your program's budget.

The next inflexible issues to be studied are production and retail merchandising requirements. This is where design plans and reality often collide, and usually it happens at a point in the process where it's going to cost someone a lot of time and money to make the necessary changes. With retailers calling the shots today on how their floor and shelf space will be used, you need to know ahead of time what physical or production constraints are going to be imposed on the program. Moreover, because retail packaging and merchandising systems change frequently, you need to keep asking a lot of questions to make sure you have the latest information. Try to take advantage of these constraints rather than just deal with them. They may even provide you with an opportunity to reconfigure your offering or sell more of your line as sets or kits.

Once deadlines and technical issues have been determined, it's time to see what financial resources are available. While creativity doesn't necessarily depend on having a large budget, it *does* depend on knowing what the budget is—*before* the process actually gets started. Trying to jumpstart design before the budget is determined rarely saves time and usually leads to false expectations. A big part of the planning process is creatively working with the budget to accomplish what you're being asked to do. In finalizing budgets, it's also important to make sure concept development and all the main creative elements (photography, illustration, copy, and so forth) have their own line-item budget amounts. It's the only way to guarantee you'll have the dollars available to implement the creative strategies you've promised.

While the inflexible issues aren't usually thought of as the place to start the creative process, having them well documented before moving on to the more subjective issues is time well spent. They are the informational foundation on which you'll base the rest of your thinking.

Reviewing Opportunities

Next on the list is a review of the creative opportunities found in the heart of the design and marketing brief. In the haste to get new products launched, it's surprising how many times critical business and marketing issues are still in flux long after the design process has started. Design shouldn't be used as a tool to try to resolve these conflicts. Before you move forward with any concept development, everyone has to agree on the answers to the big questions: Why are we launching this brand? What results do we want to achieve? The core creative concept needs to reflect and support these primary business objectives.

You also need to have a clear understanding of who you're selling the product to. Even though most products today are created for a mass-market retail environment, your concept needs to resonate with the individual personalities who make up your target audience. Is the new packaging speaking their language? Design can put a face on those markets by finding out more about them. Are they decision makers who decide what to buy, influencers who offer complementary products, or users/recommenders who already know your brand and are satisfied customers? Each of these specialized audiences has its own unique point of view on what's important when it comes to your product and packaging. What are their demographics? What needs or desires will the new product or brand satisfy? Answers to these questions will help the design team simplify the message and make the right connections. In addition, it's important to consider how consumers are supposed to interact with your packaging and product information after they leave the store. Some of the best value-added branding opportunities can happen in this post-sale environment.

Post-sale is also where the Internet can play an important role. Consumers should be able to easily access additional product information or detailed "how-to" instructions, in multiple languages, online. Creative use of this new medium will build brand loyalty by providing real value-added benefits for the consumer. It also gives your brand the tools it needs to be more competitive on the shelf. Packaging that clearly communicates the availability of additional information online has a selling advantage over brands that don't. The trick is to make sure that the experience is a good one. Don't make the consumer click through myriad pages to try to find what you promised; make it easy. Ideally, it should be a link right off the home page or a separate website devoted to your specific product offering.

Assess the Competition

Unless your product line is a completely new category, the creative review should finish with an assessment of the competitive environment. While some of the competitive issues may have been answered in the business and marketing plans, design needs to test the water with its own observations and insights of how the competition is doing. What's working for them? What isn't? Are there opportunities for this new packaging to be more effective? How do want the brand to be perceived? What messages do you want the packaging to convey? What messages do you want to avoid? What visual "tone of voice" do you want to project? Answers to these and other competitive questions will give design the opinions, observations, and concepts needed to visualize the core creative concept and, ultimately, the new visual brand positioning.

The goal is to differentiate your brand in the eyes of the consumer. We know consumers connect with brands that match their own wants and needs. We also know packaging is often the only expression of a brand the consumer sees or interacts with. That first impression has to be a good one, and your brand position needs to be immediately understood. If you've done your homework, your core creative concept will provide all the visual cues the consumer is looking for.

Kim Zarney concludes his article with an actual case study from his firm illustrating the points he has made. I am not including his case study in this book, but I would encourage readers to get a copy of the complete article from the Design Management Institute and read it.

I am in nearly total agreement with Kim Zarney. The only difference between our points of view is that Kim refers to two briefs—a design brief and a marketing brief. I would combine these two into a single brief. Although he was writing this article from the perspective of package design, the basic points are true for all design disciplines.

When Do You Need a Design Brief?

Does every design project require a design brief? Absolutely not! There are many design projects that could be classified as routine or ongoing that would not require a formal design brief. In the print world, such items as price list revisions—tent cards for meetings or trade show exhibits and so forth—may not require a design brief. But major projects in each of the design disciplines certainly do require a written design brief. Please take note: A design brief is *written*, not verbal. The most common excuse I have heard for not writing a formal design brief for major projects is that the time frame for the project was too short to develop a design brief. The second is that a written brief limits creativity. I disagree. I believe the kind of design brief I am advocating can actually enhance creativity, not stifle it. I also believe the kind of design brief I describe will ultimately shorten the time to complete a project, not lengthen it.

Let me be very clear: Verbal-only design briefings for important projects will add significantly to the time it takes to complete the project. Verbal briefings almost always lead to unfortunate misunderstandings, hard feelings, angry confrontations, major frustration, and design solutions that are not as great as they could have been.

Over the years, the constant mantras I hear from designers and design managers are, "They don't understand," "They don't give me enough time," "They don't give me enough money," "They don't let me be creative," and "They don't appreciate design!" If this is true—and I believe it often is—my answer is that it is not "they," it is "we" who are at fault. If the design profession isn't getting what it needs to do the job, shame on us. It is our fault that "they" don't understand. We haven't communicated our needs effectively. It's really that simple. It is up to the design profession to learn to become proactive—to take a leadership role—in making people appreciate and value design as a core, strategic business competency of any enterprise. Before we can even think about creating perfect design briefs, we need to understand how to talk about design as a strategic business resource, not as a decorative service.

Art versus Design

I learned a long time ago to avoid using the term "art" in any business environment. In each of my various corporate positions over the years, I joined companies with art departments, art directors, art buyers, and artists. I immediately got rid of those terms replacing them with *design department* (or *group*), *design directors, design buyers,* and *designers.* Why? Because most nondesigners do not understand the difference between *design* and *art.*

To most people, an artist is a person who is engaged in self-expression. For example, if I was a painter—an artist—and I wanted to paint a picture of a landscape, I would paint the picture as I saw it. It would be all about me and how I saw the subject. I would be accountable only to myself. I would use techniques, colors, forms, and so forth, the way I wanted to use these elements. If you happened to like my work, you might buy it. If you didn't like it, you wouldn't. However, if you did like it and bought it, then you would be wise to hire a *designer* to tell you where to hang the picture!

I believe it was the great designer Paul Rand who first said (at least, I first heard it from him), "Design is a problem-solving discipline." I recall hearing Paul Rand speak and use that phrase a number of years ago, and it has had a profound effect on my career in design. If design is a problem-solving discipline, then great design must start with a thorough understanding of the problem to be solved—which is best found in a great design brief. Though the designer may wish otherwise, the work does not revolve around him or her. Rather, the work is about finding a highly creative design solution that fits the stated problem.

Too often, nondesigners in a business setting think about design as a decorative art service: "Here's my creative idea, please make it look good." Designers who are perceived as artists are not considered strategic, business-savvy partners, but rather as clever people who draw well. I don't know about you, but as a design professional, I can't live with that perception. And so, I always worked very hard to show my nondesign colleagues that design was not art, at least in the way they defined art.

"Please Make My Ideas Look Good"

I have asked designers to bring to class examples of design briefs they currently use. For the most part, these have been written by either marketing or engineering managers, describing exactly what they are looking for from the design function. Here's one example from a marketing manager of a large houseware manufacturing firm:

> Market research has shown that in North America, more young men between the ages of twenty and thirty are drinking tea. This is particularly true on college campuses. The shift from coffee consumption to tea consumption by this market group represents an opportunity for our company to increase market share by offering a teapot targeted especially to this group.
>
> It has been decided that a teapot should be created that will appeal to young males. It must be masculine in appearance. To differentiate the product from our other teapots, it should be angular rather than round. The exterior should have a metallic finish such as stainless steel or chrome. The handle should be able to accommodate a man's hand comfortably. The spout must also be uniquely masculine in appearance.

There was more to this so-called brief. There was information about size, packaging, due dates, budget, and so forth. But the two paragraphs above are significant. In effect, the marketing group was telling the design function exactly *what* they wanted, but not necessarily *why* they wanted certain elements. To the writer(s) of this particular real example, it is clear that they were looking at designers as simply people who could execute final drawings to marketing's specifications.

I came across this brief at a small product design agency that had been asked to submit a proposal for the project. A young woman at the agency met with the houseware company's representatives, and asked a number of questions. One very important question was, "Would the agency be allowed to explore other creative solutions to the problem?" The answer was a polite no. The company executives patiently explained that they were on a fast track to get a product to market, and that the marketing group had already determined what the product should look like. Sound familiar to anyone?

This is a prime example of nondesign businesspeople not recognizing the value of design as a problem-solving discipline. It's also an example of design not being considered a core, strategic business competency. Instead, they viewed design as a decorative service for the company's ideas. The agency that showed me the brief ultimately chose not to make a proposal on this project.

Designers Shouldn't Be Taxi Drivers

Over the years, I have traveled a great deal all over the world. When I arrive at the airport in a city, I have a business problem to be solved. I am at the airport and I need to get to my hotel. As I leave the terminal building, I usually see a number of taxis waiting to take passengers to their destinations. All I have to do is tell the taxi driver exactly where I want to go. The taxi takes me to my destination, and I pay a fee for this service.

What I would really prefer is to have a transportation consultant available. There are often booths in airports with a sign that says "Information." Unfortunately, there are usually hundreds of pamphlets, but no one to speak with.

I would deeply appreciate the opportunity to explain my business needs to a transportation expert. I am the expert in my business *need*—to get to a certain destination—but I am not an expert in the best way to get there. I have time constraints, budget constraints, and perhaps other issues that I would need to explain to this expert consultant. The expert would then present me with a number of options, each with its own unique abilities to solve my problem: A taxi service will be direct, but cost more than a shuttle van. The shuttle van is cheaper, but it will probably take longer depending upon the number of other passengers in the van and their particular destinations. There is a train that is even less expensive and quite fast, but it would drop me ten blocks from my destination.

Hopefully you understand my point. Too many designers are satisfied to be simply taxi drivers. "Tell me exactly where you want to go, pay me, and I'll take you there." I don't want designers to be taxi drivers. I want designers to be transportation consultants respected for their expertise. A truly collaborative design brief process can make a major difference in the way design is perceived by nondesign executives.

That term *service* also bothers me. To my way of thinking, when someone describes what they do as a *service*, I immediately feel like I am in charge. After all, if you provide a service and I am paying for your service, I have every right to determine what it is I need from you.

Do designers provide a service? In a sense, of course we do! The CEO of a company provides a service too, but we don't call their office *CEO Services*. I advise my students to get rid of terms like *creative services*, or (worse), *graphic services*. It's a mindset thing. If you want to be considered a valued, core, strategic business competency—and one that is listened to—don't call yourself a *service*. Become a valued *partner.*

Proposals versus Design Briefs

Many companies believe a request for proposal (RFP), as well as the proposal itself, is a design brief. They are *not* the same thing. This is not to say that information in either the RFP or the resulting proposal would not be incorporated into the design brief. Most likely, this information *will* be included in the brief. It is important to understand the distinctions between RFPs, proposals, and design briefs. A great many designers I have worked with consider the RFP and the proposal all that is needed as a design brief. I argue that they are quite different.

An RFP is a document that is usually created when a business does not have its own internal design group. The purpose of the document is to give enough basic, preliminary information about a project to one or more external design resources. In turn, the external resources develop a response that outlines their approaches to the project, projected fees, time lines, and processes they would recommend to complete the work. A really good design brief needs to contain considerably more specific and strategic information. Also, a really good design brief should be developed—and written—in partnership between the design group and the requestor(s) only after considerable thought and discussion about the project.

I have also encountered internal, corporate design groups that are required to respond to an RFP. This generally occurs when the requesting group has not decided between using the internal group and taking the project to an external group. If this is the case in your company, you must handle the situation just as an external design group would. Respond to the RFP with a proposal, and then, if you have been selected to be the design partner for the project, incorporate both the information in the RFP and your response into a proper design brief.

The issuance of an RFP and the response in the form of a proposal are not sufficient to be called a design brief, simply because no dialogue has taken place between the requestor and the design group. Invariably, after the design group for the project has been identified—whether that is the internal corporate group or an external design agency—face-to-face meetings will occur that will produce more detailed information about the project than was originally offered in the RFP. This additional detail must become part of the actual design brief and the ultimate design strategy that all the stakeholders will agree on.

Design Briefs Have Many Uses

Many designers overlook the myriad uses a good design brief offers. A well-written design brief is a written agreement, or contract, between the parties involved with the project. A design brief is also a road map, if you will, that defines the various steps that will be followed from the inception of the project to its completion. Design briefs must include a considerable amount of both business strategy and design strategy. In fact, it is helpful to think of a design brief as a business plan. It is likely that most of your nondesign business partners in a design project have been to a business school. Unlike design schools, business schools teach development of business plans. This is a major reason why so many nondesign business executives believe they should create the design brief and hand it off to the design "service" group. These people think in business terms. They don't believe designers understand business strategy and objectives. If the design profession wants to become a core, strategic business partner, then the design profession must learn to think in both design and business terms. There are a great many short books on developing solid business plans. Designers and design managers should make an effort to study this topic, and approach design briefs as a combination of a business plan and a creative design strategy.

The design brief is also a project-tracking tool. Additionally, a really good design brief is an excellent outline for the final presentation of a design solution—and for making sure the project is approved! Finally, don't overlook the importance of the actual process of developing a design brief with your business partner as a tool to help nondesigners understand the often-complex phases of completing a design project.

Chapter 2
Who Is Responsible for Developing a Design Brief?

Once a valid business need that requires design expertise has been identified, and the design group that will execute the project has been determined, the process of creating a design brief must begin immediately.

The very first step is to identify who will assume "ownership" of the project. Ownership means ultimate accountability. If the project is a success, who will take the praise? If the project fails, who is responsible for the failure?

It is my strong belief that this must be *co-ownership*. There must be an owner who represents the group with the business need for the design work and a co-owner from the design function that will meet that need. They also must be *equal* partners in the project. It is a strategic business partnership, not a customer-service provider relationship.

Designers and design managers must change their mind-set from being service providers, or "taxi drivers," to a mind-set of being a strategic, equal business partner. If things go wrong, designers need to stand up and accept accountability.

Client or Partner?

Most designers and design managers I know use the term *client* (or *customer*) excessively. "My client wants a light blue background." "My client is very difficult to work with." "My clients never get me involved early enough." "My client doesn't understand design." Using this term tends to telegraph how we are approaching a project. In effect, we are saying we are not in charge of design. "They" are. Why not be partners? Why not share the responsibilities—and the accountability?

In my own consulting practice, I make a very sincere effort not to use the word *client*. Rather, I talk about "partnering" with people on a project. By strict definitions, of course, these people *are* my clients. I just don't want to think of them that way, and I don't want them to think of me as just a service provider. I want to be their partner.

As is the case with most people, I have a personal physician. One could argue that I am his client. I have medical needs; I pay him a fee for a service to meet these needs. I should be in charge, right? Wrong! If anything, my doctor seems to be far more in charge than I am. Why? Because my doctor has incredible expertise that I don't have. I am the world's greatest authority on how I feel, and my other symptoms. But my doctor is the world's greatest authority on how to solve the problem. Not me. Therefore, we are equal partners. We are both accountable for the outcome of treatment. If I haven't described my problems clearly enough or if I have withheld critical information, the doctor cannot develop the best treatment for me.

It must be the same for the design profession. We must become equal partners—equally accountable—with those people who come to us for our particular expertise, our so-called clients. When we become comfortable with this change in mind-set, wonderful, creative things can happen. Great design can happen. Working relationships can become a source of empowerment.

Co-ownership

It makes no sense to me for someone with a genuine business need for design to write a design brief and hand it to me for execution. It also makes no sense for me to write a design brief without considering the wealth of important knowledge my partner has. Therefore, many years ago, I determined there must be a minimum of two people involved in developing a design brief: someone representing the business need side and someone representing design.

There are, of course, times when there will be more than two equal partners in claiming ownership of the design brief. There could be a third. This often occurs in situations where there is a business alliance of some type. For example, two airlines form an alliance. Each retains its own brand and identity, but they jointly market some of their products. The marketing materials, which need to be designed to address these shared products, would probably require three equal partners in developing the design brief. In this example, that would mean a representative of each of the two airlines and a co-owner representing the design firm. But for the most part, two people will be all that are required as owners of the design brief. Although I strongly advocate this co-ownership of responsibility to develop a design brief, I am not advocating development by large committee, or worse, design by committee. Once a committee feels it is accountable for the actual development and writing of the brief, and for "playing the role of designer," chaos will rule. There will be a number of people on the design brief team, but only two—possibly three—should be owners. The design brief team's responsibility is to give *input* and *approve* the design brief, not necessarily to actually write it.

What Level Should the Co-owners Be?

The level of the individuals appointed co-owners of a design brief might vary depending on the scope and importance of the project to the enterprise. A senior executive and the manager (or director) of design would most likely manage an annual report to shareholders, or the design of a new, breakthrough product or service. On the other hand, a modification to an existing brochure, catalog, package, or product might utilize a mid-level marketing specialist and a lead designer as co-owners. The level of management is not really an issue. The process of developing the design brief remains the same.

Finally, there is this issue of account managers, or project managers. Many agencies employ people to be account managers—what we used to call the "suits." Should they be co-owners? I have no problem with an account manager being a co-owner of the design brief process if the account manager thoroughly understands design, the design process, and the information a designer needs. Over time, I have encountered account managers who are superb salespeople and very good process managers. Unfortunately, they didn't know much about design. In my opinion, by putting such people between the designer and the client/partner, a buffer is formed that is counterproductive to the actual realization of a great design solution. The designer must have direct contact with the person(s) he or she is developing a design solution for.

Getting Started

The first step for the co-owners is to meet one on one to determine the answers to several key questions. The most important goal of this meeting is to be sure both parties have a very clear understanding of just what this project is all about. Typical questions would include: What are the prime objectives of this project? Why is this project necessary? Why is it necessary to do this project now? What *business* outcomes do we want? What are the most critical aspects of this project? Finally—and this is most important—who are all of the stakeholders in this project? For the most part, this type of information is either not included or very vague in an RFP. This is yet another reason for not considering a RFP—and the resulting proposal—an adequate design brief.

It makes no sense to me to be a co-owner of, and therefore accountable for, a project without knowing the answers to these questions. Yet as I have been involved with design projects for all kinds of businesses over the years, it is startling how many times the answers to these questions are not clear at all. Let's take a closer look at each of these core questions.

What Are the Prime Objectives of the Project?

In nearly every case, there is some sort of working title for the project, such as "Design a new brochure for xyz product," or "Redesign of Model 1234 toaster." With all the renewed interest in brands and branding, the request I most often get is, "Can you design a logo for me?" That's all well and good. It's nice to know what we are doing. But what are the *prime* objectives for this project? What was keeping someone awake at night that generated the need to initiate this design project?

For example, is it simply because we just routinely do a new brochure every six months? Or does the current brochure contain outdated information that must be revised? Perhaps the current brochure has been ineffective in the marketplace. Why? Is the product or service new and has no brochure yet? What is this new logo supposed to convey visually? As a designer, I need to know *why* we are being asked to do this project. If I don't understand why I am doing something, I probably won't do a very good job. If design is a problem-solving discipline, then I need to know exactly what the problem is. In my career, primarily in print projects, I have been amazed at how many of my partners had to admit they really didn't know what the prime objectives were either. I would get vague responses such as, "The VP of marketing told us to create a new brochure." Or, "Sales reports the current brochure hasn't been very successful." Okay, yeah—exactly why does the VP believe we need a new brochure? Or, just what do the salespeople find is not working in the current edition?

One of the many advantages to this design brief process is that these questions can be asked in a nonconfrontational, nonthreatening environment. After all, nothing has been done yet! We are simply in the very preliminary stages of developing a design brief. On the other hand, if I wait until we are halfway through a project to ask what the prime objectives are, I will look pretty foolish. It's totally reasonable to begin with these simple questions, and to come to an agreement about the answers. If the objectives aren't clear at this preliminary meeting, it should be clear to the co-owners that the answers must be found before we go too much further.

Why Is This Project Necessary, and Why Is It Necessary Right Now?

These questions may sound deceptively simple and unnecessary, but they really are not. Timing will become a major aspect of the design brief we are about to create, and I, for one, want a good grip on the urgency associated with the project. If the urgency is genuinely great and therefore the time frame very short, this will dramatically affect the amount of time I can spend on design concept exploration and development. I need to know this *now*.

What Business Outcomes Are Expected from This Project?

Note that we are talking about business outcomes, not aesthetic outcomes. We are not doing design exploration in this meeting. Typical business outcomes may include objectives like: shorten the sales cycle, enhance competitive advantage, increase market share, firmly establish a leadership position, and so forth. Whatever the business reason for the project given, the key question from the design co-owner should be, "How?" How will this project shorten the sales cycle? How will it enhance competitive advantage, increase market share, and so forth? Your partner, representing the business side of this equation, must have some thoughts on these subjects, and you need to be certain that you are both on the same page with realistic expectations. There are times when people expect miracles from design that are just not going to happen. Design can certainly contribute to meeting these business objectives as long as you have told me what the objectives are, but design may not be able to do it all!

I have actually had marketing people say to me (too many times), "We think that if we had a really snazzy, colorful brochure that will knock people's socks off, we'll blow the competition out of the water." What does that mean? Tell me what you think *snazzy* is, and why that will make a difference. I'd also like to know why you think a snazzy brochure would give you some kind of business advantage. What quantifiable data is available to substantiate your personal opinions?

What *exactly* is the problem to be solved?

Identify Key Stakeholders

Finally, in this initial meeting, my partner and I need to identify all of the key stakeholders in this project. The list is often longer than you would think. Identifying these people up-front will allow you to develop some key strategies, which I will discuss later in the book. But it will also give you the opportunity to build these stakeholders into the phase process of the project at the most appropriate time. Let me give you some examples to think about.

Nearly all design projects today involve lawyers. There are copyright issues, intellectual property rights, trademarks, patents, and so forth. Will you utilize stock photography? If so, what kind of rights do you want for the images? Will you use external vendors or suppliers? Will there be contracts? Will a legal review be necessary prior to approval of the final design solution? It's kind of difficult not to involve lawyers in business design projects these days. They are stakeholders. (Please see chapter 11.) When will they need to be involved? How much time will they need to do their work? Is part of the overall project budget allocated to these key stakeholders for their activities? If so, how much has been allocated? Will they consult with you on an ongoing basis, or just show up at the end and tell you to make changes?

Other stakeholders include people like the sales organization, manufacturing, procurement (we used to call it "purchasing"), distribution channels, and approvers. The list will be much longer. But you don't want to find out at the last minute that warehousing and distribution have a three-month lead time to accept print materials or products into their systems! All stakeholders need to be identified up-front, then asked to provide detailed information about their issues, concerns, constraints, and needs.

Design Is Only One Ingredient of a Successful Business

Years ago, when I managed the design function at the Gillette Company, I had a mentor. We created sales collateral material, retail point-of-purchase (POP), and display materials, and worked on some packaging projects. My mentor told me that the design projects we were doing were actually just ingredients in the selling process. In order for all of the business objectives to be met, a combination of key ingredients would be necessary, but they all had to work together seamlessly. Of course, he was right. I had designers in my studio who really believed a product sold well only because of the package, brochure, or in-store display. It's always more than that. But for design to do its part effectively, the design function has to completely understand all of the other ingredients. Designers must learn to ask questions about all of these other key ingredients. What does the advertising look like, and what are the key messages in the ad? What kind of PR will be used in the sales cycle? What marketing or sales techniques will be employed? Precisely how will design support and work with all of these other activities?

One of the things my mentor asked me do was to spend a few days each year traveling around with salespeople to observe actual sales calls. I also visited retail stores to talk with store managers about how they used POP and display materials. This became an absolute priority for me over the years. How could I design or manage design for sales collateral materials if I had never been on a sales call with a salesperson from my company? As a designer, I need to thoroughly understand that whole experience. I also sent my design staff on similar expeditions into the land of the target audience. It made a huge, positive difference in our design solutions. If I wanted to be considered a core, strategic business partner, and I wanted design to be perceived the same way, then I needed to become an expert in the whole business process. Not just a "taxi" driver. Not just a service provider. Not just a clever artist.

Partners Need to Understand Each Other

The question about what the critical aspects of the project are in the mind of my co-owner is also important. If my partner believes the brochure must be very colorful, I want to know why he or she believes this is true. I want to know now, before we start the design process. If I agree with his or her rationale, all well and good. However, if I believe the door must remain open for other concepts, then I want to be able to negotiate for this creative freedom now. Doing it now will save a lot of time, frustration, and hard feelings later. By the same token, it is incumbent on me to help my partner understand the design/creative process. The partner relationship must be completely open and candid. Remember, understanding leads to appreciation!

The Design Brief Project Team

Now that the co-owners/partners have had their preliminary meeting, it is time to determine who will be part of the design brief project team. The stakeholder list will be useful to do this. Obviously, you won't be able to include everyone on your stakeholder list as a project team member. But you should be able to identify ten or twelve key stakeholders who really must be involved from the beginning. There will also be designers, writers (perhaps), and technical support people who will actually be involved in the day-to-day execution of the project. This design brief project team needs to be kept relatively small or you will never get anything done. So choose the team with great care. Be sure that the most important stakeholders are included.

Participants in my seminar on this topic often comment that they would never have the time to engage in this type of meeting. My answer, once again, is that you *have* to take the time. Whatever time you spend on this preliminary meeting will be returned to you tenfold later on. This first design brief project team meeting should only require a couple of hours of your time. Once you have established a mutually valuable working relationship with your partners, future meetings should be very brief. After you are used to working this way, you will be amazed by how quickly you can get started and how truly efficient this process can be.

The next step is to assemble your design brief project team. In the ideal world, this would be a two- or three-hour meeting with all the team members present in the same room. E-mail and other forms of technology have their places, but there is nothing like a good face-to-face discussion to get things moving quickly! I suggest two team meetings be scheduled. At the first meeting, a number of questions will undoubtedly come up that need a little time to answer. This will require a second meeting to discuss the answers to those questions. After this second design brief project team meeting, team members will stay informed through technology such as e-mail and telephone conference calls. Actually, unless there is an emergency, you may not need to assemble the whole team in one room again.

The agenda for the design brief project team meeting is fairly simple. The co-owners introduce themselves and the other team members (unless they all already know each other). Next, the co-owners review the details of the project that they discussed in their preliminary meeting. Review what we are doing, why we are doing it, what the business objectives and outcomes are, and who the stakeholders are; then identify who will actually be doing the design work.

At this point, the design brief project team is invited to comment and/or ask questions. Each member of the team should also be asked for his or her specific inputs to this project. A word of caution here. This is not a meeting to design anything. It is merely a meeting to develop scope and timing and to solicit business input. There will be questions with no apparent immediate answers. More than one person will say, "I'll have to get back to you on that." That's fine. Once again, that's why we are going to have a second meeting. The key is to be sure someone has been identified to get the answers, and a specific date for delivery of those answers has been established.

There are some ancillary benefits to this kind of meeting. First of all, everyone likes to be consulted and to feel a sense of participation in a project. At this stage, no one can really do much harm. We are just informing people something is about to happen, and their input and expertise is welcomed. Later on, you won't have to listen to people who say, "If you had only asked me, I would have told you that..." Secondly, nondesign stakeholders will begin to perceive the design function as partners, not simply decorative service providers.

Once this first team meeting has been conducted, the co-owners can go off to begin actually drafting the design brief. This first draft will be presented at the second team meeting.

Chapter 3

Essential Elements
of the Design Brief

It is important for me to repeat: There is no single, off-the-shelf format for a design brief. The actual format that you will develop on your own will vary depending on your company's standards, practices, and culture, as well as the type of design project itself (industrial design, package design, communication design, etc.). Some organizations prefer a brief that is narrative in nature. Others prefer bulleted lists. Many incorporate graphs, charts, or illustrations. Others do not. However, the key ingredients for the content of a perfect design brief are the same no matter how you format the final document.

It's also important to note that there will be times, depending on the nature of the project and the design group involved, when some of these key ingredients will not be included. There may also be some ingredients not mentioned here that you will decide should be included. At the end of the day, each organization needs to develop its own format and list of ingredients.

As mentioned in chapter 2, the co-owners actually create the first draft of the design brief and determine the design brief format that will be used. If the whole design brief project team tries to sit down and write the first draft as a committee, you will never get the brief finished.

Following the first design brief project team meeting, the co-owners create the first draft of the brief in the particular format they have chosen, recognizing that there will undoubtedly be some missing information. The first draft will be reviewed with the whole design brief project team at the second previously scheduled team meeting. This will allow team members to add their inputs and supply missing information. The goal is to have a final, unanimously agreed-upon design brief at the end of the second meeting. This process will also ensure that all critical information is indeed supplied for the design brief and that the information is current, accurate, and truly useful to everyone involved.

Of course, changes and additions might have to be made to the design brief document throughout the course of the project. This is inevitable. But by getting unanimous agreement on the essential content of the design brief prior to starting the design process, these inevitable changes can be kept to a minimum.

Having said all of that, here is a list of basic ingredients almost always found in great design briefs:

- Project Overview and Background
- Category Review
- Target Audience Review
- Company Portfolio
- Business Objectives and Design Strategy
- Project Scope, Time Line, and Budget (Phases)
- Research Data
- Appendix

Project Overview and Background

This section must clearly articulate the scope of the project, the business needs and objectives of the project, the desired outcomes, and ownership of the project.

We all recognize that many people, especially those not involved with the day-to-day work on the project, will not read an entire design brief. Therefore, this first section will also need to serve as an executive summary of the project. It needs to be rich in information without being too long or labored. It will need some careful construction. Here is an example, in the narrative format, for a major design project:

> The current company portfolio reflects a series of different visual treatments that were created at various points in time to fulfill a number of business objectives and strategies. As a result, the portfolio lacks visual cohesiveness and clarity. This exacerbates target audience confusion within the complicated and already cluttered global marketplace for these products. In order to achieve clarity and cohesiveness, shorten the sales cycle, increase competitive advantage, and improve market share—thus enhancing the bottom line—the entire portfolio must be redesigned at one time, utilizing an umbrella strategy. Design principles and strategy for future new products must also be established within this umbrella strategy.
>
> The ultimate design solution will consistently incorporate company branding elements, achieve a cohesive visual appearance across the line, and clearly distinguish the different products within this umbrella strategy.

Note that in the first paragraph, just five sentences communicate a great deal of information. The first sentence states the problem: Over time, the visual appearance of our company and its products has become fragmented. The second sentence tells us the result of this fragmentation: The portfolio lacks visual cohesiveness and clarity. The next sentence gives us more necessary information (especially for designers): The customer is confused because the industry is complicated, cluttered, and global. Next, the writers give us some insight into the business objectives of this project and a suggested solution: to redesign everything all at once. The writers also tucked in a word of advice on how to avoid the need to do this again in the foreseeable future. Finally, in the next paragraph, some mandatory elements are articulated for this redesign project.

As a designer, my head would be spinning with some initial thoughts. There will be multiple designs that all need to work together. Today there is clutter and confusion, so my concepts will need to be clear, straightforward, and simple to comprehend. I will need to develop an umbrella visual strategy. I can't change any existing brand-identity visual standards. Each product will have to include some element that distinguishes it from the other products. That's a lot of helpful input!

For the nondesign management people who will be reading this design brief, these two paragraphs firmly establish a business reason-for-being for this effort. Also, these paragraphs communicate this need in terms nondesign business partners can understand.

Following these two initial paragraphs, this particular brief went on to include some other critical information:

In order to most efficiently execute this project, the redesign will be conducted in six phases:

- *Phase 1* – Complete visual audit of existing company portfolio as well as a visual audit of the top three competitors' portfolios.
- *Phase 2* – Develop a maximum of six creative design concepts that meet project business objectives.
- *Phase 3* – Test all concepts with target audiences.
- *Phase 4* – Select three concepts and further refine each. Retest all three with target audience.

- *Phase 5* – Select one concept, fully develop it, do final testing, and prepare presentation for approval.
- *Phase 6* – Implement approved design solution.

The project has been scheduled to be complete by (<u>date</u>). The budget for this project has been set at (<u>amount</u>).

I am using a real example here, though an agreement I have with the company prohibits me from revealing its name or its competitors' names. I am using this example because it is actually very good. However, I do believe there is some missing information in the phase section, which I will deal with in some detail later.

Finally, in this one-page background section, the writers identified the project completion date, budget, co-owners, and design brief project team members:

Project owners shall be (<u>name</u>), vice president of marketing, and (<u>name</u>), strategic design director.
Design brief project team members will include: (<u>names of each of the team members</u>).

This information occupied just one single-spaced page. For many people not directly involved in the day-to-day execution of the project, this single page was as far as they read. It contained the essential information they needed. Particularly important was that accountability for the success or failure of this project was clearly established and the key stakeholders were also identified by name. It was clear to anyone and everyone what they were doing, why they were doing it, and who was accountable.

This first section may actually be one of the most difficult to write. It must be rich with information, yet succinct enough to serve as the executive summary. It will also be a key ingredient in the business objectives/design strategy, the detailed phase description, and the development of an approval presentation that will come later. In my experience over three decades of developing design briefs, this section was one of two that took the longest time to write, and it was the subject of the most debate among the design brief project team at the meeting when the brief was finalized and approved. However, it will have so many uses later that it is well worth the time and effort to get it correct now, before design work begins.

Category Review

By *category*, I am referring to the specific industry in which this product or service is involved. To many people this seems to be a "no-brainer." However, if you examine the question more closely, you will find the category—also referred to as *industry*—is not always as obvious as you might think. Perhaps a couple of examples will help.

What category is McDonald's in? Most people say "fast food." Sure, McDonald's serves fast food in its restaurants, and one could legitimately argue that it is involved in that particular category. However, it is, or originally was, *primarily* involved in the "entertainment" category. The whole concept that made McDonald's an industry leader was that it was a place for families to have fun. There were play parks, Happy Meals with games, puzzles, and small toys, Ronald McDonald the clown, and the slogan, "You deserve a break today!" The whole thing was about an entertaining time out with the kids—and "Oh, by the way, you could get a meal as well." Their primary competitors focused on the food offerings, but McDonald's brand focused more on entertainment. This differentiated them from the competition. You could eat *and* be entertained. You could have your child's birthday party there. Your children could get rid of some excess energy in the play parks. It was a strategy that worked well for the company for many years. It became a category leader. Now, if you had been asked to do a design project for McDonald's in those earlier years, wouldn't you want to know that the primary category they were competing in at the time was entertainment? Wouldn't you want to think about competition, which would include theme parks and other family entertainment venues like the circus? If you simply thought the company was about hamburgers, your design concepts would be very limited.

There are other categories that are equally important to define. For example, companies that design and build commercial aircraft are, in most people's minds, in the aircraft category. Of course they are. They need to design and build airplanes that airline companies want to buy. The airlines want reliability, capacity for specific numbers of passengers, and cost-efficiency of purchase and operation. But at the end of the day, commercial airplanes are only useful if passengers requiring transportation want to ride in them. These passengers do not perceive airplanes as machines. They want safe, comfortable, fast *transportation*. So, in this case there is actually more than one category. One is the aircraft industry. Another is the airline industry, and a third is the transportation industry. Once again, if you are engaged to do design work for a manufacturer of airplanes, shouldn't you be cognizant of the other categories you are actually designing for?

This discussion of category is often overlooked in design briefs. It really is essential. The good news is that you shouldn't have to have this discussion for every new project. Once your design team has a thorough and complete understanding of the category or categories the company is involved in, much of this material becomes essentially boilerplate. It should be included in each brief, however, and it should be reviewed and updated periodically, but after the first exploration of the topic, this section of a design brief shouldn't take that much time to complete.

More than likely, most of the information necessary for this discussion of category can be found in the company's brand positioning statement, the company's overall business strategy/philosophy statement, or the company's market research. It is essential that the category review section includes information about the competition as well as about your company. The key is to very clearly articulate a comprehensive overview of current company positioning in the marketplace. If the design solution doesn't really fit the problem it is trying to help solve and doesn't fit all of the categories the company is involved in, then it may be a good and exciting design, but not an *effective* design for that company's specific objectives.

Typical questions that should be raised in this discussion of "What category or categories are we in?" include:

1. *A List of Products.* Describe each of the products or services included in this project, their various features and benefits, current market share, and sales history. How well are they selling now? How long have they been in existence? What equity does each product have in the marketplace? Is this product or service scheduled for replacement anytime soon? How profitable is this product? Many marketing executives (and designers!) believe this is information a designer doesn't really need to be concerned about. I strongly disagree. The answers to all of these questions will go a long way toward helping me find creative, and appropriate, design concepts that will meet the company's business objectives. It is essential information to help me focus on possible design directions.

2. *The Competition.* Create a similar list for the major competitors.

3. *Pricing and Promotion.* Describe pricing and promotion methods used for each product or service, as well as their competitors. Be as specific and detailed as possible.

    Early in my career, when I wasn't very concerned about these things, I learned a critical lesson. My group was asked to design a package for a new consumer health and beauty aid product. We actually came up with a "winner," as we were wont to say in my design group. Unfortunately, when we presented our design solution for approval, it was quickly rejected. Why? The product was going to be promoted by distributing free sample sizes in home delivery of local newspapers—a fact we had not been aware of and neglected to even ask about. The sample sizes were quite small so that they would fit in the newspaper bags, and our design just would not work on the scale of a free-sample size. We had to start all over again, this time keeping the various product sizes in mind.

I have also seen many design solutions that were "over-designed" for the price point range of the product. The cost of implementing the design solution would seriously affect the ultimate price that had to be charged for the product. Designers need to know everything possible about pricing and promotion techniques *prior* to beginning development of creative concepts.

4. *Brand.* Relate all of the individual products or services to the company's brand strategy and positioning. Do the same thing for the key competitors. What is the perception of your brand vis-à-vis your competitors in the marketplace? What are the most significant differences in those perceptions? How important are they? For example, I did some work for a company that was more than 150 years old. It was an industry leader. Then a new start-up company emerged and became a key competitor. The new company presented itself as modern, up-to-date, leading-edge, and reliable. The key question, of course, was, How much of the somewhat old, well-established brand equity should we leverage in meeting this new competitor head on? Do we move toward a more contemporary visual approach, or stay with the tried-and-true? This was not an insignificant—or easy—discussion. But it was an essential discussion to have prior to beginning any design exploration.

5. *Category (or Industry) Trends.* What significant trends are occurring in this category? How might these trends affect this project? For example, several years ago, when I designed for the health and beauty aids category, shampoo products were a key source of revenue for the company. The trend had been for shampoos to have a color—predominately green or amber. This trend, of course, influenced our

color palettes for projects. And then the trend shifted. "Clear" became the new trend. Consumers responded better to shampoos that were "clear as rainwater." Green and amber were out, clear was in. Now, clear is a difficult element to deal with in a color palette! Obviously, all sorts of category or industry trends will influence design solutions in a major way.

6. *Company Business Strategy.* Just what is the business strategy the company is currently pursuing? Is it price? Quality? Value? Environmental correctness? Or, the business strategy may be driven by acquisition, partnerships, or alliances. Whatever this business strategy is, the design function has to be fully aware of it. If the design function isn't aware of the ways in which the company intends to generate revenue and profit, then the design function is not able to effectively design solutions that support that business strategy.

Target Audience Review

In the hundreds of design briefs that I have reviewed, the target audience review is the most often understated section of a design brief. Too often, the audience is actually described in just a few words. Some examples include: "women, eighteen to thirty," "mothers," "teenagers," "shareholders," "executives," and the ever-popular "everyone!" I would need to know a great deal more than that. What *kind* of women eighteen to thirty? Where do they live? What level of education do they have? What are their interests? Does "mothers" include grandmothers? Young mothers? Mature mothers? Stepmothers? These overly simple target audience descriptions tell me nothing useful about the people I am designing for. If there is a genuine business need for a design project and a desired outcome, then I need to know precisely who I am designing for.

Therefore, it becomes essential to describe all target audiences as completely as possible in the design brief. Pay particular attention to national, cultural, regional, and gender differences, especially for global offerings. Just exactly who will be looking at and responding to your design?

Earlier, I described my habit of visiting customers on a regular basis in order to get to know and understand them in greater depth. If, for some reason, this practice of visiting your target audience regularly is not practical in your design group, then you must rely on input from people who do know the target audience from first-hand experience. For the most part, this will be the company's sales force. Designers must forge strong relationships with those people who regularly come into contact with the target audience(s). Don't be afraid to ask as many questions of these people as you need to completely understand the audience.

Also, keep in mind there are usually multiple audiences—not just one. Going back to my aircraft manufacturer example, designers must understand the various levels of target audiences. First, the aircraft has to be attractive to the airlines that will purchase the airplanes. Next, the airplanes will have to be attractive to prospective airline passengers, as well as to the crews who fly the planes. These passengers are male and female, business and leisure travelers, young and old. Each of the target audience groups has very different needs, and designers have to understand all of these needs. The simple description of "everyone" in the design brief doesn't even begin to tell the story adequately.

Global offerings are even more difficult. A favorite question that designers debate constantly is, "Can you develop one design solution that works equally well anywhere in the world?" My answer is usually no. Geographic variations are usually required to accommodate the needs of the various cultures and backgrounds of the target audiences.

At one point, I had the opportunity to speak with some designers from a major greeting card company in North America. They were explaining the complexity of designing greeting cards for various parts of the continent. For example, Christmas cards in New England need to look quite different from those that people will purchase in Arizona. Tastes, traditions, local décor, and climate were all factors in determining the design elements for these holiday greeting cards. To meet this challenge, the company routinely sent designers to visit all regions of the North American continent. The objective was for the designers to experience firsthand the visual preferences, traditions, and tastes of these various regions. It was the only way the company could ensure that its design staff was creating appropriate designs for each audience. Now, a greeting card company is highly dependent on design. In effect, it is their product. So the investment in this practice makes good business sense. Other companies may not see it that way, so you may have to explore other ways to get regional target-audience data.

In today's complex, global marketplace, great designers need to understand all audiences, and to be certain they have that understanding before beginning the design process. A comprehensive target-audience description is absolutely critical.

Company Portfolio

The company portfolio is particularly vital when an external design agency is working on a project for a business. However, it is also a valuable section for in-house design groups. Once again, this is one of those sections of a design brief that initially may take some time to develop, but once created, it can become boilerplate that is inserted into all subsequent design briefs. It should be reviewed fairly often, and updated when necessary.

This section describes the company (or enterprise) and its activities as completely as possible. Just what are all the elements that make up the organization? How critical are each of these various elements to the project being described in the design brief? For example, Ben & Jerry's Ice Cream, a major U.S. brand, made a strong commitment from the beginning to be known as a socially conscious and responsible enterprise. The founders contributed a great deal of money from their profits, and provided a variety of services, to a wide range of charities and worthy causes. In fact, this was a key element of their business philosophy and strategy. In this case, it would be critical for a design group to take this philosophy into consideration when developing design concepts for the Ben & Jerry's organization.

In other cases, it might be more of an issue of total understanding of the firm's brand positioning and brand reputation across all of its offerings.

If the organization uses a monolithic brand strategy, using a single master brand for all of its offerings—as, for example, IBM has traditionally employed—that monolithic brand strategy needs to be reinforced and clearly articulated in the design brief.

On the other hand, if the company employs a branded strategy in which each product or service is branded separately, then the unique attributes of that brand would need to be included in the brief. Procter & Gamble employs a branded approach. Often, consumers are not even fully aware that Tide, Crest, Dawn, Joy, Pampers, and so forth, are P&G products because they are all positioned as discrete, stand-alone brands. Many companies employ this strategy so that they can actually compete with themselves. For example, P&G's Dawn and Joy brands are both dishwashing liquids, yet they have different brand identities and brand characteristics. Whichever one you decide to purchase, P&G still gets the revenue.

There are also companies that utilize an endorsed branding strategy. General Motors is one example. They have several brands—Chevrolet, Buick, Cadillac—each with its own brand identities and positioning but all presented as a GM product. This is a typical example of a tiered approach. GM's brands range from the lower end of the price range to the very high end, with the luxury brand Cadillac on top. While each of its brands has distinctive attributes that must be conveyed visually, the master GM brand remains the same for all sub-brands. Therefore, the challenge is to effectively differentiate Cadillac from Chevrolet, but to also consistently present the GM master brand and all that it stands for.

Finally, there are companies that utilize some of each of the above. The Gillette Company has some monolithic brands (Gillette), and some branded (Braun, Duracell, Oral B). If you were asked to partner in a design project for Oral B, you should confirm what part, if any, the parent brand, Gillette, needs to play in the design solution.

The critical issue is to be sure the design brief very clearly indicates the ways in which this particular project must be integrated—or not integrated—with the rest of the company portfolio of products and/or services.

This particular section, along with several other sections in a comprehensive design brief, can be a valuable tool for initiating very important and meaningful discussions among your design staff, as well as with your nondesign business partners. Having these kinds of discussions prior to beginning the design process often leads to real inspiration for enhanced creativity.

Business Objectives and Design Strategy

In my experience, the business objectives section has probably been the most important section of a design brief. Yet it is also the one section that is most often left out!

For a design solution to be truly effective, it must solve the problem. If there is a problem, and a solution is required, then it follows that not only must the problem be clearly stated, but the business objectives of the solution also have to be clearly articulated. Once there is a clear understanding of the business problem and its objectives, then—and only then—can a coherent design strategy be developed.

In the first section of the design brief, the project overview and background, we laid the groundwork for the business objectives. Now is the time not only to expand that discussion but also to formulate a plan of attack, a strategy, for approaching the design process.

All of the key stakeholders in a project need to be in agreement with this section. This is your "contract." If done well, it is your best opportunity to obtain agreement to experiment and pursue a variety of creative concepts. It will also become a key ingredient in preparing your final presentation of a design solution for approval and acceptance.

As previously stated, you will undoubtedly want to develop your own format for a design brief, but as a starting point, let me share with you the format I used for this section for many years.

My co-owner/partner and I would create two columns. The column on the left was headlined Business Objectives. I made it clear to my partner that he or she was the sole owner of this column by writing, "Please list, in priority order, all of your business objectives for this project." Since I agreed that my partner was the world's greatest authority on the business needs for the project, it only made sense to initially let him or her develop this list.

The column on the right was mine under the same ground rules. This column was headlined Design Strategy. Since we were the world's greatest experts on design in this effort, my staff and I would develop some specific design strategies that would allow us to meet each of the stated business objectives. Please take note: At this point I am talking about a design strategy, a direction, rather than describing very specific design concepts. The design concepts will ultimately emerge from the strategy.

Once a draft of both lists was completed, my partner and I would review and discuss each item one by one. To be candid, this would often lead to some sticky questions and disagreements between us, but since the design process had not yet started (remember, we are just *developing* the brief at this point), these discussions and disagreements were not confrontational, but rather highly productive.

Once my partner and I had agreed to the content and substance in each column, we reviewed it with the entire design brief project team to get their *buy-in*, or unanimous agreement, with the brief.

There are many advantages to this process. First and foremost, it helps to speed the whole process up, believe it or not! While it is true that this section of the brief may take a little longer than others to create, it does provide focus and clarity for the design concept development stage, and thus compresses the time for this important phase. It also nearly completely eliminates a lot of misunderstandings throughout the entire process. And misunderstanding meetings use up a lot of valuable time! In addition, this section is an educational tool for both parties. The designer or design manager is able to get a better understanding of the business problem, and the folks with the problem to be solved through design get a better understanding of design process and concept development. It's a win-win scenario.

What happens if, during the early stages of the design process—the concept development stages—the designer(s) suddenly come up with a brilliant and highly creative concept that does not fit with the agreed-upon strategy in the brief? No problem! Design briefs can be revised during the design process, provided that the revisions reflect a better solution to the design problem, and that the co-owner/partners and design brief project team all agree to the changes. In a sense, a design brief—like many other business plans—is a living document. It's okay to revise, when necessary. The important point is, if the design brief is very carefully thought through and written, these inevitable changes will be minimized, once again saving valuable time. When either there is no design brief, or a brief is created with minimal information, that is when valuable creative time is lost in the race to make a deadline.

Refer back to Kim Zarney's stir-fry analogy in chapter 1. It's most helpful to have all your "ingredients" assembled before beginning to cook! Our goal is to always be sure we start out with every bit of information the design team really needs to create a brilliant and effective design solution, with a minimum of wasted time in those countless meetings about what people personally "like" or "don't like." This is the section that provides a good, strategic road map to find a truly creative design solution.

Project Scope, Time Line, and Budget: The Phases

This part of the design brief provides critical detail to the road map to success we are creating. It ensures that everyone involved has a clear understanding of, and is in agreement with, every aspect (phase) of the project. It also serves as a wonderful device for the design team to educate its business partners on design process. It can often lead to successful negotiations to get more time and budget for the project as well.

Creating this section provides the design team manager with the opportunity to break a design project down into its various discrete parts. By doing this, your partner begins to understand some of the detail involved in executing the project. Once we understand things better, we are usually able to appreciate them more! Many designers I speak with say things like, "Why doesn't my client understand what I am trying to do?" "Why can't they understand how long it takes, and how much it costs, to do these projects?" Well, this is your opportunity to change all of that!

Too often the design profession seems to keep its processes a carefully guarded secret. As a result, many nondesign businesspeople tend to think we just go in the back room, get creative, and come out with something that looks really good. That "artist" mentality again! By sitting with your partner and working through the project in phases, you will have the opportunity to educate your partner and to get acceptance for your time and budget requirements in order to complete the project successfully.

To accomplish this, the description of each phase must contain, at a minimum, the following items:

- Precise description of the phase (activity)
- Time frame for the phase
- People who will be involved in the phase (be sure to include key stakeholders such as IP lawyers, purchasing agents, market researchers, and so forth)

- Approvals of the particular phase (who, when, where, etc.)
- Budget for the phase

The number of phases will, of course, be determined by the specific project. The critical thing is to be sure the description of the phase is complete and understandable to everyone involved. The best way to proceed is to first create the ideal scenario *with* your partner. You will recall our earlier example from the project overview and background section of the brief. In that real example, six phases were summarized.

This brief summary is fine for that particular overview section. But now is the time to add more detail to the description of each phase.

Returning to our particular example, phase 1 was summarized as a "complete visual audit of existing company portfolio as well as a visual audit of the top three competitors portfolios." Okay, this is a logical starting point. But now is the time to expand the discussion of this phase with your partner.

- Do we have an example or examples of all current artifacts in the company portfolio? If not, precisely who will gather this material? How long will that take?
- How about the competitors? Do we know who the three are?
- Do we have examples of their current materials or products for this audit? Who will provide these examples? How long will it take for them to provide these materials?
- Who will actually be involved in conducting the audit? What criteria should we apply to this audit?
- How will the results be presented? Who will they be presented to? How long will this part of the audit process take?
- What costs are involved to do this piece of the project? What are the start and end dates for this phase?
- Will this phase require any stakeholder involvement or approvals? If so, who will those people be?

I have often found that in this example of an audit process, my partner is blown away by the scope, effort, time, and expense that is involved. They are usually surprised that design concept work really shouldn't start until after the audit has been completed and the design team has analyzed the results.

When you complete the analysis for each additional phase of the project with your partner and add up the costs, the total will likely show that more time and money are required than originally planned. Your business partner will probably be trembling. This is the point where the design project manager says, "Okay, let's go back to each phase and see where we can make some cuts." For each suggested cut, you must ask each other, "What are the *business risks* of eliminating, or not fully funding, this activity?" Notice that I am saying "business risks." If you simply say, "The design team won't want to eliminate this step," then your partner can say, "It doesn't matter what the design team wants!" But if there is a business-related risk that could potentially affect the project's business objectives, it will be more likely that your partner will agree the cut shouldn't be made. What usually happens during this process is that an agreement is reached to provide more time for the project, redefine the project's objectives, provide more funding, or all of the above.

What is occurring is a businesslike discussion of what is really required to achieve a specific business goal. The process is educational for your partner because he or she is a participant. It is very hard to disagree with something you have helped to create in the first place! As you do more and more of these with various partners, each begins to have a greater appreciation for the needs of designers and the design process. Once again, we have a win-win scenario.

The Last Three Phases

As previously stated, the phases are largely determined by the specific project and also by the type of design involved. For example, a product design (industrial design) project might involve a variety of engineering elements and model building that would not be part of a project to design a print piece, such as a brochure. Therefore, the industrial design project will probably have additional phases not found in a design brief for a print project. But I strongly recommend that all design projects, no matter what the specifics, include the following three final phases: 1) final approval of project, 2) implementation, and 3) measurement metrics.

Clearly, every project will have to face a final approval phase. The brief should include details about this phase. When will the approval meeting occur? Who will ultimately have final approval authority? Who will make the approval presentation? What is the budget for creating the approval presentation? Many times people forget that creating a presentation for approval has some costs related to it. This must be included in the overall project budget. These presentations also take considerable time just to create.

The issue about who will make the presentation can be a sticky one! From my point of view, it should always be the co-owners—the partners who have accepted accountability for the results of the project. However, I am aware that this is not always the case. There are situations where someone else who is not directly involved throughout the process ends up taking the solution and presenting it to the final approver. Although I disapprove of this practice, it is used in the real world! In these cases, the best you can do is to create a bullet-proof presentation for approval, make that presentation to the person who will be taking it forward on your behalf and hope that he or she will use your materials effectively. If your approval presentation is compelling and complete, two things might occur. One, you will be asked to at least attend the presentation as an observer, or two, you might even be asked to present anyway. No matter what your situation, be sure to describe the approval process in the design brief. I will focus more on creating presentations for approval in chapter 8.

Just because a design solution is approved doesn't mean the co-owners and design team can walk away from it! Once approved, the design has to be implemented. This might involve a manufacturing or printing process. It certainly will involve some type of distribution process. After all, you have done this project for a target audience. How does it get to them? The implementation is as much a part of the design project as concept development and refinement and must be part of the complete design brief. This is a place where many of the stakeholders you identified in your preliminary meeting will come into play. Procurement (purchasing), print production, sales force, warehousing, distribution, and so forth, might all be critical components of implementing your project. Specific dates and budget figures must also be included in the implementation phase description.

Finally, the last phase should always be measurement metrics. How will anyone know this design solution, this design project, was successful? Remember, you and your co-owner/partner have accepted accountability for the success or failure of this project. What criteria will be applied to this measurement process, and how long will it take? Is there a cost involved in the measurement process?

There are many ways to measure results of a design project. Again, it depends on the type of project. If you have designed a new product, did it sell? If it was a new package design, did it increase sales volume? The key to determining just how to measure the results of design is to go back to the project's business objectives.

You will recall that up front we asked these questions: Why are we doing this project? Why are we doing it now? What are the desired outcomes? What are the business objectives? The answers to these questions provide the basis for measuring results. If the desired outcomes and business objectives were achieved, the design project was successful!

Research Questions

Research questions are the next-to-last major section of the complete design brief, but may or may not be required by your organization.

I am including it here because, once again, it is an area often overlooked. During the initial discussions with the design brief team, it is quite likely that a number of questions will go unanswered. If the answers are really critical to the success of the design project, then it is best to list those questions in this section, determine who will get the answers, figure out when he or she will get the answers, and ultimately include what the answers were. One area that always needs to be included is the research that will be necessary by your IP attorney. Some issues, such as trademark registration and patent application, may take considerable time. This section, if required, is simply a safety net to ensure that all critical questions are addressed, answered, and provided to the designer(s).

Appendix

An appendix is also an optional section of a design brief, but one that I always include. This is where you put all that stuff that doesn't seem to logically fit in the other sections. It might contain documents that summarize research data, competitive analyses, news clippings, photographs, other visual materials from your audits, or materials simply gathered for inspiration. In my career, the appendix was often a file box full of such things, including thumbnails created during the concept development stages. This appendix could be important enough to include with the hard copies of the design brief, or—as in my case—just a single file box full of various materials that is available to anyone on the design team or the design brief project team.

It was not unusual during my time as a corporate design manager to embark on a project and have someone say, "You know, this is similar to the project we did three years ago, remember?" In those cases, the old design brief and my file box appendix to that brief often saved us a lot of time and effort in creating the new design brief for the new project.

Some Final Words about Content

In this chapter, I have covered what I believe to be essential elements of content for a really useful design brief. This does not mean that you may not wish to add other topics for your brief, nor does it mean that you must necessarily include each of these items. At a minimum, I would suggest you at least *consider* every one of these essential items. If, after consideration and perhaps debate with your co-owner/partner, you decide to eliminate one or more of them, that is okay. At least have the discussion before you decide.

If the category review doesn't seem necessary to you for a particular project, eliminate it. But be careful. It is of paramount importance that the whole design team understands what is currently going on in the industry and what the competition is doing. Don't ever simply assume everyone is up-to-date on this information. Industry trends move very fast these days. Likewise, the company portfolio section may seem unimportant to you for a particular project. But at least bring the topic up for consideration. Research data and an appendix may also be optional. It all depends on the particular project.

I firmly believe that all of the sections of a design brief are important. Some, however, are particularly critical to any business enterprise. Below is my list of essentials any good design brief can not go without:

- The *project overview and background*, which becomes the executive summary, to clearly define the project and its objectives.
- A comprehensive discussion of *target audience*.
- Discussion of how *design strategy is matched to business objectives*.
- The *phases*, which includes a discussion of the project scope, time line, and budget.

Among the most critical elements of the design brief are the sections dealing with the initial design strategy developed to meet the business objectives and the phases. These two sections, in particular, will get your project launched on a positive note.

Even though only the co-owners will write the first draft of the brief, this does not mean that you can't have separate discussions about all of these items with your design team prior to meeting with your partner to write the draft. In fact, I made this a regular practice. Once I identified the designer(s) who would be involved with a particular project, I would sit down with them and go over all of the information gathered from the preliminary meeting with my co-owner, as well as the preliminary meeting with the whole design brief project team of key stakeholders. We would pay particular attention to the business objectives, then develop a draft of our accompanying design strategy as a design team. Just as I am opposed to a business function just handing a design brief to a design group, I am also opposed to just handing off my own thoughts about design strategy to the designer(s) who will actually be doing the work with no further discussion. Designers need to be involved in formulating the design strategy for the project. Once the design team and I had reached some agreement, I would then sit one-on-one with my partner to write the draft of the brief. I am aware of some groups who bring the entire design team to this meeting to draft a brief. The problem that often arises with this practice is that the co-owner is then also entitled to bring some people from his or her function to this meeting. Now we are back to writing a draft in a committee setting. This invariably takes much longer.

I realize that this process I am recommending appears to be a very lengthy one! To be honest, the first few times you use this method of creating a design brief, it will take longer than you had hoped or planned. But keep a few things in mind. Number one, the extra time you spend in this up-front process will more than be made up later. Also, as you do more and more projects using this process, they will become easier and faster. As I mentioned before, many of the items in the brief will become boilerplate and only need to be dropped into the next new brief. Your target audience, company portfolio, and category review may not change very much from project to project. However, it is important to update these sections as required.

You must also keep in mind that this is an educational process. You are beginning to eliminate some of those common complaints I hear design managers and designers repeat day in and day out: "They don't understand." "They don't give me enough time or budget." "They don't get me involved early enough." You are beginning to communicate your needs as a design professional effectively in terms that nondesign business partners can understand.

Finally, this is the best way I have ever found to move design from being a decorative service to becoming a genuinely respected core, strategic business partner. The design brief process can help you make this shift in thinking. Will this new appreciation for the added value of design happen instantly? Probably not. It will take some time and additional effort on your part to make the transition. I never promised it would be easy. But I have also said it is up to the design profession to be proactive, to take a leadership role, and to make the necessary changes in order to elevate our profession to the place where we want it to be.

Chapter 4
Getting the Design Brief Approved

Once you and your co-owner/partner have successfully created a draft of the design brief, and once you have determined a specific format that works for your organization, you will need to finalize the brief with the whole design brief project team made up of key stakeholders.

This will involve some careful planning between the co-owners/partners. What you do not want is an extended process of rewriting the draft in a committee meeting! It is my experience that the best strategy is to circulate copies of the design brief draft to team members only. Allow them a relatively short period of time—no more than five business days—to review the document. Make it very clear that this review is to detect any glaring errors or omissions *only*. It is *not* a meeting to discuss design concepts as a group. If at all possible, schedule a face-to-face meeting of the team. Two hours should be more than enough time. If not everyone can attend, ask those who can't appear in person to submit their written comments as least one day prior to the meeting. Distribute these written comments from those who are absent to the whole design brief project team. Then be sure to discuss the absentee's comments. If you don't do this, you are opening the door to criticism later from the absentee team members. You don't want to allow them to say, "I sent you a list of concerns in writing, but the whole team never saw my comments." Always remember that this process is inclusive of key stakeholders.

Purpose of Final Review

There are actually multiple purposes for this final review of the design brief. First and foremost, you want to be sure that there are no factual errors. You need to be sure that the data on category (industry) trends is accurate and up-to-date. You want absolute clarity about the target audience(s). The decisions regarding the relevance of the company portfolio to this project need to be verified. After that, you are really establishing buy-in, especially the business objectives, desired outcomes, and design strategy section, as well as all of the details of the phases (particularly the time allocated to each phase and the budget for each phase). There will undoubtedly be some discussion about each of the design brief's sections by team members. The co-owners/partners have the responsibility of explaining, and if necessary, defending, each section of the design brief in business terms.

The appendix, if you have one at this point, may or may not need to be included in this circulated draft. If the appendix contains essential information that everyone on the design brief team needs to review, by all means, include it. On the other hand, if it's essentially a collection of materials intended as inspiration for the design team (described in the last chapter), then it may only really be useful to the designer(s) who will be working on the project. This is something that you and your co-owner/partner will need to decide.

This process will once again provide the design manager with an opportunity to demonstrate that design is a problem-solving discipline, and not simply an exercise in aesthetics. It will reinforce the fact that there is a business need for the project that will be approached in a strategic, businesslike manner by the design team.

Side benefits include the fact that a large number of people—the key stakeholders—will feel some ownership and direct involvement with the project, and realize that they are being consulted from day one. This fact will also become an important ingredient in your final presentation for approval.

I recall an approval presentation in which a senior manager expressed surprise that we listed so many key stakeholders who had been involved from the beginning. His exact words to me were, "I thought this stuff came about because of the whim of some designer on your staff." The fact that a thoughtful, inclusive, strategic, businesslike process was involved went a long way toward getting quick approval for our design solution.

The Approved Brief

Your goal at this point is to get the design brief approved quickly so you can begin the design work. Because I am a highly cautious individual, I always asked the whole design brief team to sign or initial the brief. I would also make it very clear that the inevitable changes to the brief—although we planned not to have many—would have to be run by the whole team before any revisions would be made.

Once the approved design brief was in place, I recommended sending copies to the wider group of stakeholders we had identified in the initial meeting but did not include as design brief project team members. This would certainly include all approvers mentioned in the phases, as well as the final approver. Occasionally, one or more people on this distribution list would actually read the entire brief and submit comments. At times these comments were negative or disapproving. If the points were indeed valid, we would implement our revision process. Often they simply represented personal, highly subjective opinions or suggestions about what the design should ultimately look like. Many people cannot resist the temptation to try their hand at design and therefore offer a number of their personal design ideas!

I remember one individual who read the brief and then suggested, "You should use a lot of stars on the cover as a symbol of our 'stellar' product line." It is not prudent to allow design to become a committee process. In these cases, my co-owner/partner and I would send a cordial acknowledgement thanking the person for their input, emphasizing that this was a team effort and that the team would strive to make the best possible decisions based upon the stated business objectives and desired outcomes. We would also remind the person offering this kind of input that there was an approval process stated in each phase that would provide an excellent safeguard against the project failing.

In time, by initiating this type of process, your business partner will recognize the value of design to the success of the business, and the design function gains more credibility and trust. This leads to fewer challenges to design briefs in the future.

As the design manager, I would meet separately with my entire creative team for the project and go through the approved brief in great detail. Although I had consulted with the design team before drafting the brief, they were usually not involved with the design brief project team approval process for the final design brief.

Because I was involved with print projects for most of my career, writers were always closely associated with our design projects. I would absolutely include the writers in this team meeting of creatives involved with the project. In fact, in two of my corporate positions, the writers were part of my group and reported directly to me. For many high-level print projects, I would also invite a representative of the printing company to this meeting. I did this because over the years, I have learned that printers can often offer very helpful input if they are consulted early in the design process.

Other design disciplines may require different kinds of expertise during their particular design process. Ultimately, the design manager will need to determine just who he or she feels should be a part of this creative team review of the approved design brief.

In-House versus External Design Agencies

In those cases where an external design firm was engaged to do the design work, I followed the same process. In most cases, one of the co-owners/partners in the creation of the brief will be a representative of the external design firm. Other organizations wait until the design brief is finalized before selecting an external design agency to do the work. I don't approve of this practice. I feel strongly that a design brief should be created as a partnership between the requestor and the design function. This is what a request for proposal (RFP) is for.

As mentioned before, the RFP and the resulting proposal should serve as the basis for creating a real design brief once the contract is awarded to a design agency. To me, it is counterproductive to present a finished brief to any design group—in-house or external—without the design group's collaboration.

This is a sticky situation in many companies. I have worked with a number of businesses that have no internal design group, but that do have project managers employed to represent the company and supervise the work of external design resources. For the most part this situation exists because—once again—companies are not used to thinking of the design professionals as business-oriented strategic partners. They believe they need a business-savvy manager to direct the work of the "art service." If these project managers are not trained in design, I would strongly recommend creating an RFP, evaluating proposals, identifying the external agency, and then making the agency design manager the co-owner/partner to write the brief. After all, we have already said that the co-owners are the people accountable for the outcome of the design project. It is not possible to be the co-owner/partner for design, and be truly accountable for the ultimate design solution, if you are a project manager with no training in design!

Chapter 5
Using the Design Brief

The design strategy provides a clear starting point for the design team to begin developing creative concepts for the project. As all designers know, inspiration is more difficult to find than most people realize. The design strategy column should help get this inspiration process going. For example, I had the opportunity to work with a company that, quite frankly, had a major credibility gap. In their zeal to garner attention (really a perceived competitive advantage), they had a habit of announcing breakthrough products they were developing well in advance of actually having a working prototype of the new product. As is often the case, the product took much longer to develop and perfect than they had anticipated. Having announced something that wasn't a reality yet, they tended to produce drawings, or illustrations, of what they were working on for announcement literature. Over time, the marketplace for their products became very skeptical of these breakthrough product announcements. The firm finally realized that this business practice was actually harming their brand image.

The firm's management decided they needed a brand-new, very different-looking catalog. Among their business objectives for this catalog was an objective to signal that they were not only innovative but also credible. One of the design strategies listed in the brief opposite this business objective was, "to explore concepts that would use only actual photographs of products, being used by real people." Drawings and illustrations would not be appropriate since those devices implied the products were only in the conceptual stages. This simple design strategy immediately signaled to the design team that: 1) "reality" had to be a major ingredient of any concept they would explore and 2) this was clearly a major strategic concept departure for them.

It was somewhat amazing to me (and also very gratifying) that when the small group of designers had their initial meeting to discuss the design strategy, there was a rapid flow of some very creative concept ideas. They were immediately inspired and excited about the various possibilities that were put forth. Not a bad way to get a project off the ground!

Having a well-thought-out design strategy prior to beginning a project will save a great deal of time at the outset of design work. In fact, it will save much more time than it took to develop the strategy in the first place! Some designers worry that having to adhere to an agreed-upon design strategy in the design brief will limit their ability to develop creative design concepts. What if a concept suddenly emerges that doesn't fit with the design strategy in the brief? What if that concept is a real "winner"? This doesn't have to be a problem at all. Remember, we have a process to revise a design brief. There is no harm in discovering a better design strategy or concept during the design process. The key is that this exciting concept must still meet the business objectives of the project. It must still be an effective design *solution* for the problem, not just a pretty work of art.

Another way in which the business objective/design strategy section works for you is that it provides a benchmark, a checkpoint, for evaluating initial concepts, as well as evaluating the further development of those concepts. As concept development progresses, the design team is able to quickly refer to this section to be sure it is on the correct track. For years, designers have said that there is really no way to measure graphic design in business terms. Well, there is. You must continually ask yourself, Are the initial design concepts meeting the stated business objectives? If so, why or how? This also provides realistic criteria for quick approvals of each phase. It makes the approval process completely objective, rather than subjective. It should eliminate the dreaded comment, "I don't like it!" Once again, personal opinions can't really be challenged effectively. If a person says, "I don't like it," he or she is telling the truth.

Design is, by its very nature, somewhat subjective. As the old saying goes, "Beauty is in the eye of the beholder." This simple fact is one of the several reasons the design profession has had many difficulties over the years. While art may be almost totally subjective, design should not be. So how do we change this perception of design as decoration (or art), which is very subjective? By not allowing discussions about design to wander into this highly subjective area of personal feelings.

I used to set up a "norm" at the outset of meetings to talk about any design issue. The norm was that no one in the room, including me, could use terms such as, "I think," "I believe," "I feel," "I like," or, "I don't like." Try it. It's a very difficult thing to do! I would explain simply that those terms were highly personal and therefore not really relevant to the business. You "like" blue, I "like" red. So what? We are both telling the truth. That is how we feel. That is what we "like." There can be no winners, or significant progress, in such discussions. However, objective comments give you basis for objective evaluation and productive discussion ("Blue works best to solve this problem because…" or "This concept is not working to solve the particular problem because…")

Whenever anyone says to you, "I don't like it," simply acknowledge his or her honest feelings, and then take the discussion out of the subjective arena and return it to the objective. "I understand you don't like it personally, but what is it about this concept (or color, spacing, border, etc.) that is not working to solve the business problem?" When I have done this, I have often found that many individuals can't really tell you why it's not working. It simply does not suit their particular taste. This is when a design professional, an expert in the field, has to explain in businesslike terms why a concept or design element *is* working to solve the problem and meet the business objectives. If you allow the discussion to stay in the realm of subjective opinion, I can almost guarantee the design function will lose the debate!

The Phases

The phase portion of the brief that includes project scope, time line, and budget works for you as a road map through the project. There are a great many ways to track a project. Some design groups do it more or less manually, while others use a variety of software packages designed to keep track of project details. I am particularly impressed with a system developed by a company called Workflow by Design. Their electronic tracking systems have been adopted by a number of major companies.

However you do it, there seems to be no question that, at the end of the day, businesses want to be able to track progress—and expenses—for *any* project, not only design projects. The phase section allows the design team not only to determine if it is on time and on budget but also to be certain that key stakeholders are not forgotten. If a legal review is necessary at certain points, has that been scheduled? When must manufacturing be brought into the process? Have they been notified? Such details are often forgotten or put off until the last minute, causing troublesome delays in the project.

I have found that involving many stakeholders in the early phases is a good idea. There really isn't much harm anyone can do to a design project in its early phases. Stakeholders involved early on tend to feel more included and are therefore less apt to raise significant objections later, as the project is coming to a conclusion. Traditionally designers have tried very hard to keep nondesign stakeholders out of the process because when these folks start to actually see what you have been up to they immediately want to be critical. It's human nature. On the other hand, if they have been included from the beginning, they are "with" you. I'm not suggesting that they should get to play designer. I'm really just advocating not keeping everyone in the dark until the eleventh hour. Let them see where you are, being careful to explain in very clear, nonsubjective, businesslike language just what you are doing and why it is working to meet the stated business objectives. Hardly anyone reacts well to surprises.

You will also find some truly helpful input at times. Take manufacturing input, for example. Printing is, of course, manufacturing. I know of a situation where the design team felt that foil stamping of an image on the cover of a brochure would be a perfect solution. However, the budget just wasn't available. By bringing in their printer (a stakeholder) early in the process, rather than just before they were ready to go to print, they learned of a brand new printing technique that essentially provided the look of foil stamping but without the added cost. They were able to achieve the effect they knew would work best to meet the business objectives after all!

Another key ingredient in the phase description has to do with approvals of each phase. We all know how frustrating it is to try to go through what seems like an endless chain of approvers for a design project. Part of the problem is that most design groups wait until they have a design solution that they really believe in before they start showing it to various approvers. You know what happens. A lower-level approver asks you to make some minor changes, and you do. The next level of approver does the same thing. You make some minor changes again. This sometimes goes on for several layers of approvers. At each level, you make alterations. It doesn't take very long for your design solution to be so fragmented that it no longer works. However, by involving some of these lower-level approvers in the early phases, particularly in the initial concept development and refinement stages, you will actually be able to minimize their further involvement later. After all, they have already approved their portions prior to the point where the ultimate decision is made by the key approver at the end of the project.

Testing

Finally, I like to include some testing in most phases. Everyone in the immediate family believes the newborn baby is the most beautiful being ever to inhabit the earth. It is prudent for you to get some outside opinions. You and your design staff are probably too close to the design project to be truly objective. I tested with a sampling of the target audience(s) during the initial concept stages, and again as we closed in on a preferred design solution.

How can you do that? The quickest and easiest solution is to go directly to your target audience—the people you are designing for. Once we had three or four concepts we were comfortable with, I would call the sales office and ask if I could travel with a salesperson for an afternoon. I promised not to interfere with the sales call; I simply wanted a few minutes with the customer—our target audience—at the end of the call to show him or her some comps of our concepts. Without going into any detail, I would simply ask the customer to react briefly to each concept. What immediate response did he or she have to each treatment?

Customers actually love to be asked to do this and are very candid in their comments. Of course, many times the design group's direction was validated. But there were those instances when our favorite concepts just didn't play well with the customers. Clearly, we were on the wrong track. Better to know that now, in the concept development or exploration stage, than later! Is this method of testing scientific? No, absolutely not. But I did find it quick, inexpensive, and valid enough to provide us with a sanity check.

We would use slightly more formal testing techniques with the target audience later in the project, when we were near the point of finalizing a design solution to the problem. Our goal with this testing was to determine if we had really met all of the stated business objectives and desired outcomes described in the design brief.

Target Audience

The target audience section is another part of the brief I would invest some time in discussing with the design team. Clearly, the designer(s) need to know everything possible about the people their design work is aimed at. With in-house design groups, this may have been done so many times that the design staff is already very familiar with the target audience. In fact, that is one of the reasons in-house design staffs can often complete projects that meet the business objectives in shorter time frames than an external agency can. But if you have a number of relatively new people, or are using an external design agency that may not be very familiar with your target audience, then by all means, invest the time in this discussion prior to starting the project.

All information about the audience is critical to designers. This is one reason I can't stand simple phrases like, "women, eighteen to thirty" or "executives" as the only description of the target audience in a design brief. It is not enough, in my opinion. To become a strategic business partner and a core business competency, designers need to understand the customer as well as—if not better than—everyone else in the company.

Using Other Sections of the Design Brief

One of the reasons I strenuously object to minimal design briefs, or worse yet, entirely verbal design briefings, is that essential reference information for designers is not always apparent. When things are written down and are as complete and detailed as possible, everyone involved, from designers to nondesign stakeholders, is singing from the same sheet of music. The complete design brief provides everyone with a common reference point for continued discussions and exploration of truly creative solutions. If new information or creative concepts emerge during the active discussion periods, so be it. Revise the brief. Just be sure everyone involved is aware of not only the revisions but also the reasoning behind the revisions.

The various other sections of the complete design brief allow the design staff to know as much as is humanly possible to codify the project's business needs. The category review, the company portfolio section, the research data, and the appendix become critical reference tools for each designer working on the project. If the appendix happens to be rich with visual samples—often photographs or competitive literature—it can become an important time-saver in the inevitable early "discovery" process.

All sections of the design brief should be discussed openly and thoroughly with the creative team. This is especially true if many of the team members were not involved in the actual writing of the brief. Having a written document provides the basis for and a solid tool for facilitation of these creative discussions.

Such "perfect" design briefs enhance the creative process, become an invaluable reference tool, and allow the whole design process to proceed expeditiously without a great deal of confusion and bickering among the stakeholders and the creative team. Remember, great design briefs also become valuable archival documents that can be reviewed in the future when similar projects come along.

Finally, as I have mentioned previously, the design brief will become your outline for creating a design solution approval presentation. I will discuss this in some detail in chapter 8.

Chapter 6
Competitive Analysis

I mentioned earlier that a thorough visual audit should be done of your key competitors' products, packaging, and collateral materials. Collection and audit of these materials on a routine basis should be mandatory for all in-house design groups. External design agencies often need to scramble rather quickly to get a handle on a new client/partner's competitors. (This is yet another reason why I believe in-house design groups generally have an advantage over external design agencies.) If you are going to produce a truly creative design solution to a business problem, then you need to know not only everything you can about the target audience for your design but also what other visual communication this audience is receiving on a regular basis from your key competitors.

While it is true that most large corporations invest a fair amount of time, money, and human resources in competitive analysis, their competitive analyses rarely include a visual design audit. Instead, they assemble a wealth of information about audience demographics, market share, cost and profitability analysis, sales figures, stock value, and a myriad of other very important business considerations. This is all well and good. Corporate design functions need to have access to all of that information. In fact, design groups need to be sure they are informed of this data on an ongoing basis and that they study and analyze this data.

However, the design function will invariably have to do its own visual audit and analysis of competitors' design solutions. Design can clearly demonstrate an added value to the enterprise, not only by conducting these visual audits and analyses on a regular basis, but also by sharing the results of this activity throughout the organization.

The Most Common Approach

The most common approach to the process of competitive analysis is to assemble everything you can find from the competition and integrate it with your company's visual materials or products. You should know which competitors are doing really well in the marketplace and why. Is it pricing, value, elegance, availability, or a combination of those—and possibly many others? More importantly, how are these competitors using design for competitive advantage? What design elements are working very well for them, and where are the weaknesses?

In print, we used to have a large room (we called it the War Room), where we could pin up all the competitive literature on the walls. We did a design audit with just the design staff, then invited representatives from sales, marketing, and all other key stakeholders to join us for a discussion of the results of our visual audit. For many of these stakeholders, this was a new experience. Most of them admitted they had never really given that much thought to design as an element of competitive advantage. To them, it seemed to be too subjective to really pay much attention to.

We invited these key stakeholders to this meeting to add their observations to our own. We were particularly interested in any feedback from the target audience that they could provide that related to the visual manifestation and communications of our competitors. I wanted the design team to know everything possible about the competition before it began to develop concepts for a project. Just what would be necessary to effectively differentiate our company's products or services from the competition visually? This type of discussion was always very helpful to the design team and, once again, helped save precious time later in the design process. Designers were now veritable experts about what was going on in the marketplace that, these days, is often very visually cluttered! I also made it a point to collect samples of national, regional, or geographic variations of designs used by key competitors. This was particularly important if we were designing for a global audience. In the last few years, an increasingly critical element to include in a visual audit of key competitors has been their websites.

Partners from other nondesign disciplines cannot help but be impressed by this type of strategic thinking from design. Although our partners from marketing and sales often had excellent knowledge about the marketplace, the demographics of the audience, pricing, distribution techniques, and many other things, the various design elements and techniques that supported the competitive offering(s) were not part of their expertise. The design function demonstrated clearly that we could bring a unique and strategic added value to the table. This helps the design function move further ahead in becoming a valued, core, strategic competency in the business.

Just once in my consulting career, I encountered a client/partner who held the opinion that competitive analysis was not important. The CEO of the company believed that his organization was the market leader and therefore that everyone else should try to copy them. His instructions were, "No time or money should be wasted studying the competition! Let them study us." I simply cannot agree with this point of view. It seems somewhat arrogant to me. I urge you to do regular visual audits and design analysis of your primary competitors. You don't need to wait for a specific design project to begin this work. It should be ongoing.

I have interviewed a great number of CEOs during the course of my consulting career. I am continually amazed by how many of them really believe their existing customer base is completely loyal to them. Many of these CEOs have told me that their loyal customers would never even think of buying a competitor's product. Then I go out and do my target audience interviews. What the customers actually tell me is that they are quite happy with a certain company's product or service, but if something more interesting, more appealing, or better came along, they would more than likely give it a try. The target audience for most businesses is often rather fickle. I maintain that being aware of what the customer is seeing in the marketplace, and of how your competitors are presenting themselves visually and verbally, are key ingredients that must be fully understood before beginning the creative design process. Therefore, a comprehensive, visual, competitive analysis is critical to the process.

Assembling Competitive Material

So, just how do you get all of this competitive stuff to audit and analyze? It can be a very laborious and expensive process. This is why I recommend collecting competitive materials on an ongoing basis. One of the very best, least expensive, and fastest methods is to be sure design group staffs attend all major industry trade shows. In fact, I believe design group staffs should be right at the top of the list in any corporation to attend industry trade shows. Think about it. Where else can you enter a large room, be handed a free plastic bag, and wander around picking up literature from every major player in the industry? When your bag is full, they will even give you another one, free!

In one day—possibly in only a half-day—designers can pick up all of the relevant and most current literature from key competitors. It could take a year or more to collect that much intelligence from other sources. Many trade show operators also allow attendees the opportunity to take photographs in the exhibit hall. When this is permitted, designers can select what items (aside from literature) they would like to record on film or digitally. This might include the exhibition booth itself, products, and so forth. A clever person can also do a little eavesdropping and listen to the "pitches" made by competitors to prospective customers visiting their booth.

There is nothing illegal, unprofessional, or immoral about this practice. If you pay the price of admission, you are entitled to visit all of the exhibits, though you will probably be required to wear some type of identification badge that identifies you as a competitor. Your competitors in most cases may be reluctant to be overly cooperative with you, but they cannot deny you the ability to look around and take notes! Trade shows are an absolute visual gold mine for competitive analysis of design.

Another good source for competitive materials is the company's sales force members. As they come into direct contact with customers every day, and presumably have good relationships with their customers, they can often pick up competitive literature from the customer. They only need to know what you need, and of course, why you need it. This is also a way for design to begin a relationship with the sales force. You will appreciate every ally you can have in the company. If you are designing for a global audience, ask your various regional or country managers to supply you with examples of competitive literature or photographs of products from your competitors in their own geographies.

When conducting your visual audit, make notes and sketches of all the salient design elements of your competitor's materials. These will most likely end up in the appendix. The specific design details may not be as relevant to nondesign stakeholders, but they will be critical to your design staff.

No matter how you decide to assemble competitive information, include the process as part of your design brief. Build in time and budget to actually collect the information, if you don't already have it, and for the actual visual audit process. This activity should be described completely in the phase section of the brief.

Chapter 7

Establishing Credibility
and Trust for Design

I would like to pause at this point to address a question I'm sure is on every reader's mind. "Everything you have been saying so far sounds good to me, but in my company (or my client/partner's company), design is not considered an equal partner, and design is not regarded as a leadership group. Also, we are never given enough time to do all of this. Just how are we supposed to institute this new process?"

Fair enough. At best, design has been traditionally viewed as kind of a necessary evil in business. Businesses know they need the training and skills of a designer, but they often wish that wasn't the case. In my DMI seminar, Managing Design for Strategic Advantage, I ask each participant to prepare two slides to share with the class. On the first slide, I ask them to provide a list of words that describe how they see themselves as designers or design managers. On the second slide, they are asked to do the same thing, but this time they must indicate how they believe other managers in the company perceive them. For each slide, I also ask them to include some type of image that reflects the contents of the slide. The results have been fascinating! (Many times I have wished that I saved all of these presentations. They would make a wonderful short book!)

With very few exceptions, the first slide includes phrases like "creative," "miracle worker," "talented," "fast," "overworked," "underpaid," "not appreciated," and "lifesaver." The images are traditionally something like an octopus with many tentacles, or a downtrodden, tired genius.

The second slide always contains phrases such as "difficult," "slow," "well-meaning," and the ever-popular "necessary evil."

What is always interesting to me is that in the more than five years I have been doing this exercise with students, there are always two slides. No one has ever said, "I only did one slide because the way I perceive myself is exactly the way others perceive me." One brave student had only a blank slide for the second slide. She simply said, "I don't think management really has any perception of me or what I do at all!"

But students always report a disconnect. "I am rather wonderful, and I work miracles for the company, which are never appreciated. The company sees me as a necessary resource, yet they won't listen to me or give me enough time or money, and they don't ever include me early enough in the process." What's going on? Why do designers feel they are so misunderstood? Why are they not included early on in the process, and why aren't their opinions valued? The answer is really very simple. Traditionally, designers have no credibility as business-savvy people, and as a result they aren't trusted enough to make critical business decisions.

I recall one person's presentation at a seminar very vividly. The young man explained how he added flavor, spice, excitement, and effectiveness to each of his print projects. He went on to say that his work contributed enormously to the success of the company. He told the group that he was "gourmet" and symbolized this with an image of basil. On the second slide he indicated that nondesign managers felt he was difficult to work with, didn't complete work fast enough, and was not willing to listen, but agreed his design solutions were quite good. His final comment, accompanied by his second image, of parsley, was, "They think I am very decorative, like parsley sitting on the side of the dinner plate, but that I'm not a significant part of the main meal!" I really enjoyed his presentation because it summed up, in a humorous and creative way, what I hear all the time: "I know I'm good, but nobody really appreciates me."

As I mentioned in chapter 1, "they" are not at fault for this disconnect—"we" are. If there is a major difference between how we see ourselves and how we know others are seeing us, then we are not communicating effectively. It is up to us to change this dynamic. It will probably take some time. You can't just walk in Monday morning and say, "I read this book over the weekend, and now we have to change the way we do design briefs. I am now your equal partner, accountable, and co-owner of the process. It's going to be great!" No one will believe you have had such a miraculous change over the weekend. Rather, it will take time and considerable changes in the way you work with people to get to the point where you have enough credibility and trust to be considered an equal partner and genuine co-owner of the design brief process. You will have to work hard to earn a seat at the table. But the good news is that it *can* be done—and many have done it.

The Model

It seems like everyone who embarks on a career to teach "how-to" seminars has developed some kind of model to illustrate critical points. So that's what I have done as well. The following is meant to be a visual guide to the process. I have found it works effectively for designers and design managers who want to improve the perception of design, and the design function, in the corporate world.

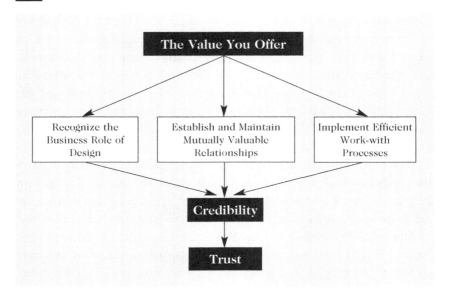

Permit me to expand on each part of this model.

The Value You Offer

This is the most critical—and therefore the first—step in my model. If you don't understand why you are valuable, or why design is valuable, then no one else will either. Many of us believe we know why we are valuable, but knowing it and communicating it effectively are two entirely different things. I would hasten to add that what we believe makes us valuable is not always what others believe is of real value. In the aforementioned exercise with the two slides, the types of things people most often list on the first slide are not the things nondesign corporate managers, particularly senior managers, are looking for. The items I routinely see on the first slide are merely what senior managers have come to expect from any employee. Being a person who gets work done on time, with very short time schedules, is a given to them. Staying within budget is also expected. Being very creative? Well, that's why they hired you in the first place! Being able to handle multiple projects at the same time? They do the same thing—everyday. And the list goes on.

Designers tend to list the "tactical" things they do everyday. There is seldom anything remotely "strategic" on the lists I see. To be truly valued, an equal partner in the process, and a core, strategic business competency, design and designers must learn to speak the language of business, and relate what they do to business results. If you want to be a co-owner and equal partner in the design brief process, for example, then you must communicate and demonstrate clearly that you are thinking strategically about the effects of design as a solution to the business problem. If your focus is entirely on aesthetics and tactics, you will never be perceived as a full partner. Rather you will be the "decorator," the "art service." Not that aesthetics and tactics will not play a significant role at the end of the day; they just can't be all you talk about.

When I say "the value you offer," just what do I mean by "you"? In the context of this model, two things. There is you personally, the individual who will be an equal partner in a process. And then, there is the collective you, the design function as a whole. You want the design function to be valued and respected as a critical component of the whole organization, and you also want to garner respect and trust as the manager of the design process.

Paradoxical Leadership: A Journey with John Tyson

I have a good friend, John Tyson, whom I respect and admire greatly. John was trained as an industrial designer. Up until his retirement about a year ago, John was vice president of Nortel's (formerly

Northern Telecom) Corporate Design Group. Yes, you are reading that correctly—vice president! Very few design managers ever become vice presidents of major corporations, but John Tyson did. He was able to get to this position because he understood how to effectively communicate the value of design.

In "Paradoxical Leadership: A Journey with John Tyson,"[1] by Artemis March—an article written for *Design Management Journal* a some time ago, but certainly as relevant today as it was then—Artemis interviewed my friend John Tyson and included several quotes from John and others in his group about how they transformed the design function at (then) Northern Telecom. Artemis March is a consultant and educator who facilitates organizational transformation. She has directed dozens of field-based studies of companies for universities and business clients, including Chrysler Motors, AT&T, IBM, and Johnson & Johnson. Because the quotes from Artemis's article are so pertinent to what I am talking about in discovering and communicating the value of design, I have excerpted portions of her article here.

Excerpt from Design Management Journal, *by Artemis March*

Paradoxical Leadership: A Journey with John Tyson

Northern Telecom's top management came to the conclusion that design was very underleveraged at Bell Northern Research (BNR) and its R&D subsidiary, and that the industrial design function needed to be reinvented if Northern was to achieve industry leadership in digital telecommunications. Wondering if John Tyson, then vice president for Market Development in NT's transmission group, would be interested in taking on this challenge, the CEO told him, "I'm thinking of doing something with your old group—something big." Tyson's first reaction was, "It's probably not big enough."

Tyson's "old group" was Design Interpretive, the internal design group he had founded in 1973, a few years after he joined NT as its first industrial designer. But by 1983, he had opted out of design. As he explains it, "I got tired of talking about design and pushing. I decided to go to the other side and pull. On the other side, they don't value design. It's largely invisible."

Tyson's response to the CEO's "feeler" was vintage Tyson. Peter Trussler, who joined Tyson's Design Interpretive in its early days and is now director of the Corporate Design Group (CDG) which evolved from it, recalls that Tyson's confidence and free spirit were expressed as openly back then as they are now:

> When John first joined the company, they couldn't find a classification for him, so they labeled him a draftsman. He said, "Take that off or get yourself another designer. You don't understand where my value is."…He would call a meeting with the president and think nothing of it, because he was concerned with the value of the meeting, not the protocol of hierarchy.…He's not adverse to risk. He loves a challenge. He always has a very interesting way of coming at things. And he has always been that way. What you see is what you get. That's what's valued in this corporation. I think it reflects well on us that a person like that has been welcomed and valued, that he's not been chewed up and spat out. When there's a crisis, or a need for fresh ideas, or for someone to challenge things, I think a lot of people start wondering, "What's Tyson up to these days?"

Now, as you can see, John Tyson was not a shy, reactive design manager. John clearly understood that a major part of his role, and the first step to success, was to communicate clearly the value of design. Another portion of this article details how John Tyson approached the task of reinventing design at Northern Telecom.

In the three months following his return to Design Interpretive, Tyson and his senior managers worked their way through a six-step "reset" of the design function. Tyson described the process as a journey in which "each step delivered the next one." The first step was the decision to reinvent the design function as a center of excellence. Once that decision was taken, the group knew it had to write a meaningful policy. Next, it changed the funding structure. The fourth step was defining the program, and that in turn drove the new organizational structures and processes. The final step is referred to by the group as "the pudding"—as in "the proof of the pudding is in the eating."

One of the most frequently used words in the group's lexicon is "value." CDG people are constantly considering its meaning and how to translate it into product: What is value? What do users value? What is our value? How do we create value? They also talk a lot about accountability, and what it means for how they work together. This ongoing, evolving dialogue was generated and is nurtured by the core concept around which the reset evolved: that design was to be a center of excellence.

Although this concept cannot be pinned down in a precise mechanical way, Tyson's metaphorical language suggests that a center of excellence emerges from a dynamic, sometimes dialectical, process of the holistic convergence of accountability, value, and leadership. As he explains,

"If you are a center of excellence, you're accountable." Accountability means that "we're accountable for the value we contribute to the corporation."

When he describes what assuming accountability for delivering value really means, it becomes clear that Tyson is a leader who thinks in paradoxical or dialectical terms. Disputing the view that accountability is about who's in control, he says, "To get control you have to give it away. We give it away. The value accrues to our partner. We invest in our partner." He observes that, by contrast, "most people operate as if value accrues to themselves. But the value of the work you do accrues to your partners, and to the user or chooser of the product."

The center of excellence concept is strongly underlined in CDG's new policy statement. In contrast to most book-size policies, Tyson and his managers wanted something very concise that would capture the spirit of the new organization. On the day the reset was announced... a carefully crafted one-page policy statement was given to the group's members. Signed by top management, the policy validates CDG's status as a corporate center for excellence, responsible for driving design excellence and continuity across all NT products. It acknowledges that the design group has signoff authority at all "gate reviews" in the new product introduction process, and that it is on a par with its partners in product marketing and product development in contributing to "new product definition, conceptualization, specification, and final design."

Tyson and his managers crafted a policy statement that concentrates on what CDG will *give* to the corporation. Design makes itself accountable for delivering a "leadership focus" and a "strategic driving force" for delivering "outstanding customer value...and product continuity" in order to "effectively contribute...to world industry leadership." There are no contingencies, no back-door escapes. Tyson describes the document as "a license that simply empowers you to be the best there is. It also says, "Today I am different than I was yesterday. Now I own this. I'm accountable for it." And that's why we had to change the name of the group [from Design Interpretive to the Corporate Design Group]." Although he had named the design group Design Interpretive, "it became evident in the journey that the name had to change....What mattered was the metamorphosis."

I wanted to include this small excerpt from Artemis March's article on John Tyson because it describes how one design manager successfully communicated the value of design to his corporation. Each design group will need to develop its own plan for "resetting" perceptions within the organization. It's hard work, but worth the effort.

An Exercise to Get You Started

There is an exercise that works very well for getting to the heart of this value business. You can do this alone to determine your personal, added value to the business, and you can do the same exercise with your design staff to come up with ways in which design as a function adds value to any enterprise. The technique is identical either way.

Make a list of every reason you can think of that either you—or the design function—add value to a business. Write down every single thing that comes into your mind. Don't worry at this point about elegant wording, or even relevance. If it comes to mind, write it down. More than likely you will create a fairly lengthy list in very short order. That is always gratifying. I have seen people look at the long list they just generated and say, "Wow, look at all the stuff we do so well!" Put this list aside for a while. Maybe a day or two. Then take it out again and work through the list item by item. Ask yourself for each item, "Does this really, really matter to nondesign businesspeople? Do they really care?" If the answer is no, then draw a line through the item. I have done this exercise hundreds of times with groups. Let me give you some admittedly extreme (to make the point) examples of items that had to come off the list: "I am really an expert with typography," "I am able to keep many details in my head encompassing multiple projects," "I am friendly and easy to work with," "I use white space very effectively." In a way, all good stuff, but completely meaningless to a business.

I wanted you to put everything down that came into your head for this first pass, because when you draw a line through those items that are really irrelevant, you will have a visual record of the kinds of things you are saying every day that most nondesign people really don't react well to.

Now is when the excitement about how long your original list was evaporates. You are going to end up with a much shorter list than you expected.

Next, try to work the list again. But this time, do not simply jot down everything that comes into your head. Focus on those items that nondesigners would perceive as truly added value. Also, pay more attention to the words you are using to describe each item. This step will take considerably more time than the first go-round. But the results should be equally as exciting. The list will be shorter, but the content will be rich with information about just how design brings added value to a business. Think always in business terms— not aesthetic terms. Just what can design do for a business?

Some of the rather strong items I have seen on this second list include: "We shorten the sales cycle." "We visually differentiate our company's products or services in a cluttered marketplace." "We create a powerful competitive advantage." "We clarify the company's business strategy through visual means."

This is the stuff that will make senior, nondesign business managers sit up and take notice. One rather compelling (if also somewhat nonconversational) statement I have seen is: "We are responsible for the visual manifestation of the company's overall business strategy, as approved by the board of directors and the shareholders." That doesn't sound like a simple decorative service to me. It sounds more like a statement from a strategic business group—and that's what you want to become.

Once you have discovered just exactly what your added value really is, begin to incorporate these thoughts into everything you do. Some groups, as John Tyson described, actually develop a "design philosophy" from this exercise. Use these powerful strategic business ideas in memos, presentations, meetings, everyday conversation, and design briefs.

You will often have chance meetings with people in the company who don't know you. Inevitably, they will ask what you do. I try this in class, asking students to tell me what designers do. The first word out of their mouths is almost always, "Umm?" This is followed by something like, "I do design work for packages (or whatever)." Then they stop, not really knowing where to go with the answer to this question. After doing this exercise, you should have a whole arsenal of things firmly implanted in your mind that will capture the attention of the person asking the question. Down deep, what you want is for them to become aware of the importance of design to the business, and you want them to say, "I had no idea, I thought you guys were just artists. We should talk some more!"

Many human resource professionals describe a technique called the "two-minute drill." These people argue that in an interview situation, the first two minutes are critical to the outcome of the interview. You must be able to communicate, succinctly and in a compelling way, just what it is you have to offer that is unique. By taking the time to determine the real, added value you offer as a design professional, you will also be able to learn to communicate this value in two minutes or less. It will take some practice, but it is an important component to changing the perception of design in the business world.

To be truly valued in the business world, you absolutely must know what your value is (and we are all valuable!), and you must be able to articulate it clearly and simply in business terms at the drop of a hat. If you really aren't very clear on just why you're a valuable asset, no one else will ever get it either. Before moving any further through the model, do this exercise. It makes a wonderful agenda item for a design staff meeting. Everyone in your group needs to have the same understanding of your added value. And it beats the hell out of dreary staff meetings where all that happens is each designer gives an endless list of status reports!

An Initiative from One Design Manager

I did a workshop for a group of graphic design managers. The workshop primarily addressed the things I have just been writing about. One of the participants mentioned that his group had established a tradition of each member of the design staff doing an original piece of poster art at each holiday season. A theme would be chosen, such as snowmen at Christmastime. Using that theme, each designer created a single piece of artwork that was then displayed on the bulletin board outside of his or her office. The gentleman reported that all of the employees enjoyed looking at the various creative results of the staff.

Of course, what this group was unknowingly doing was reinforcing the idea that the design group consisted only of clever artists who drew interesting pictures! After the workshop, I received an e-mail from this manager. Here's what he told me:

> I found a lot of useful information in this workshop that I am beginning to implement. I met with my staff and briefed them on the day, as you suggested. One of the things we decided to do is to remove the "artistic self-expression" posters we have plastered on our walls and replace them with framed examples of our best projects, with a brief tag that identifies the business objective and how we accomplished the business objective using design. Next, we will design a large

wall sign, typography only, with key words that describe our new mantra: "The Corporate Design Group believes Good Design is Good Business. Design Partnerships + Business Objectives + Design Strategy = Optimal Business Results." We will also display some of our meaningful awards, and some before-and-after examples of our work, all framed with explanations.

Obviously, that e-mail made my day! The design manager has subsequently reported that employees of the company were blown away by this display. What this group has done is taken a very positive step towards communicating the value of design as a core, strategic business competency. And they are doing it in a highly visible, strategic way.

Recognize the Business Role of Design

"Recognize the Business Role of Design" could also be turned around to say, "The role of design in business." Either way you say it, every designer or design manager doing design projects for a business must understand how design adds value to that business. Remember, design is a problem-solving discipline. If your design activities are in support of a business of some type, then the problem to be solved through design will be a *business* problem. Just how far, and in what ways, can design contribute to the solving of a business problem? The answer is, "In more ways than most people think!"

I have a very close friend and colleague who told me very bluntly that at the end of the day, design really couldn't do very much in terms of solving real business problems. My friend is a brilliant business strategist, particularly in the finance arena. He insists that design is necessary only as a vehicle, or environment, to contain information about the company's products or services. His view is not only commonly held but I would say prevalent in the business world. There are a few companies, of course, whose success depends completely on design. For example, greeting card companies, which I mentioned earlier. These design-oriented businesses tend to have a built-in appreciation and respect for design. But they are the exceptions.

It is the responsibility of the design profession to change this perception. Frankly, we have done a lousy job of it for years. In order to communicate the role of design clearly, as well as its value, we must first understand the role of design in business.

Just what are the business problems your company (or the client company you are partnering with) is facing? Ask yourself, "What is keeping the CEO awake at night? What are the business issues that are most troubling to him or her?" Then ask yourself, "In what ways can effective design play a role in solving this problem?"

Let me use an example to illustrate the point. This example is real, but once again I have had to disguise it somewhat at the request of the company. (Remember, companies do not like to air their dirty laundry in public!)

A Consumer Electronics Firm Example

Harry is the head of design for a major manufacturer of low-cost consumer electronics such as televisions, VCRs, radios, and so forth. Harry's group consists of industrial designers, package designers, and graphic designers responsible for all of the collateral literature for the company. Although the company is located in Asia, their single largest market is in North America.

The company slowly built a rather significant market share by focusing on the low end. Their products were among the least expensive in their categories. They primarily sold through mass-market discounters such as Kmart and Walmart. Although the products were inexpensive, they did function in a very satisfactory manner.

But the world changed. Due to increases in manufacturing and selling costs, increased tariffs for export/import, and the need for higher margins to satisfy the shareholders, it was no longer possible to maintain their traditionally very low prices to the consumer. The dilemma senior management faced involved changing consumer perception to ensure that the new higher prices at retail would be accepted by their target audience.

The CEO was under a great deal of pressure from the board of directors to maintain not only profitability but also market share.

Senior management held countless high-level meetings to try to develop a strategy for effectively repositioning the brand in the marketplace. They engaged a well-known management consulting firm to help them develop a strategic plan.

Harry, the head of all design activities for the company, was aware of the dilemma and the high-level meetings, but he was not asked to be a participant. He anxiously awaited the results so that he could determine how the new strategy and positioning would affect design in the organization.

This is, unfortunately, a very common scenario: designers being separated from business strategy, or designers waiting for someone to tell them what the business strategy is, so they can react appropriately. In this case, Harry should have been proactive. If he had clearly understood the role of design in this business crisis, and had been able to communicate that role clearly to the CEO in business terms, then he might have been invited to sit at the table and be part of the strategic solution, rather than an after-the-fact service provider.

Certainly, there are myriad ways in which design played a role in this business problem. The problem called for a fresh look at the design of the products themselves—certainly the packaging—and the brand (and sales) collateral. It should have been clear that all aspects of design would have to be revisited with the intent to reduce costs without sacrificing potential profit and market share. I interviewed Harry, and he told me that he simply didn't have enough business training to fully engage himself in these high-level meetings. He told me that he was a designer and a design manager, not a financial wizard! Well, you don't have to be a financial wizard, or an MBA, to understand the role of design in this kind of problem. The whole problem would never be solved solely with design. Design can do very little about increased export/import tariffs. Design can do very little about increased costs of employee salaries and benefits in the manufacturing plants. But design can do something about costs of raw materials by specifying different materials. Design could eliminate some costs in packaging and print materials. Design can play a major role in presenting the company brand in a more effective and positive way to the target audience.

Harry was too concerned about managing the aesthetics of design and not concerned or involved enough with the hard business issues. As a manager of such a large design organization, he had a duty to be proactive and bring the design component to the table.

If you still think design is not really an important component of any business, try this exercise. Get a hold of the company's organizational chart. Don't worry about the names of individuals on the chart—focus on the various functions. For each function, list all of the ways that that function uses design, whether you are responsible for the design or not. The rule is you cannot skip any function on the chart. What you will find is that design does play a meaningful role in each and every function of every business. Every function! If that doesn't demonstrate the role of design in any business, I'm not sure what will.

I have had people argue that there are functions in a business that do not require design. Take warehousing, for example. Well, are there signs in that warehouse? Do the employees wear uniforms? Are there various forms and documents used to track materials coming in and out of the warehouse? Aren't all of those things designed? How about employee food services? Do they have menus? Is the company brand printed on napkins and trays? I think you get the point. Design plays a role in *every* facet of any business. Businesses could not survive or function without design. Once again, let me make it clear that I am not advocating that every design group actually do all of the design so essential to every business function. What I am advocating is that the design function be recognized as the experts on design and should therefore be considered the strategic business center for design.

Often during my corporate career, I would call the manager of a particular function, introduce myself, and offer to attend a future staff meeting of theirs to explain how design played a role in their piece of the business. Often, they were not even aware that they required design on a regular basis. They never thought of design in that way. At the staff meeting, I would take perhaps ten or fifteen minutes to point out how design played a part in their work, and then I would offer to be a consultant if needed on issues they had that involved design. I could help food service find a good resource to print the company logo correctly on napkins, for example. I didn't offer to do the work, just to help them do it well, and correctly, through other resources. This practice accomplished several things:

- It helped large numbers of people understand that design played a role in their daily lives.
- It gave my corporate design function wide visibility.
- It established my design function as a center for expertise.
- I was able to learn firsthand what business issues each function was most concerned about.
- I was able to develop allies all over the company—mutually valuable relationships, if you will, that always served the interests and needs of the design function in future projects. For example, it made the process of listing all stakeholders in the design brief a great deal easier. I was on the way to becoming a transportation consultant rather than a taxi driver.

Mutually Valuable Relationships

Creating mutually valuable relationships all across the enterprise not only for the function of design but also for the design manager is critical to becoming a strategic partner. However, it is probably the most neglected aspect of the design function I encounter on a regular basis! Designers and design managers seem to have a difficult time in reaching out and being proactive in a business. Let me give you another real (although somewhat disguised for the reasons noted previously) example.

A major, global, high-tech company, in the race to keep competitive and still be a market leader, acquired a smaller company to create a new division and offer some innovative new products. As part of the purchase agreement, the smaller company's founder (and president) was made president of the new division and promised a great deal of autonomy in running the division. He was a brilliant engineer and business manager and knew that he had only one year to show a profit or be replaced.

The new division head went to a former college classmate of his who ran a small design firm and commissioned him to develop a division logo, product logos, packaging, and some communications collateral material. The design manager of the parent corporation did not find out this work was going on until after it had been completed. The new division's materials bore absolutely no relationship to the parent corporation's house style, and, frankly, were outstanding examples of very mediocre design.

The parent corporation's design manager had a meeting with his boss and complained that the new division's material was not acceptable and that his group should have been involved from the beginning. The design manager's boss patiently explained that the new division president had to move very quickly, was promised autonomy, and had no time or budget to go back and do the work over again. He suggested the design manager just let the whole thing drop.

What Went Wrong?

First of all, this is becoming almost an everyday occurrence. Mergers, acquisitions, partnerships, and alliances between companies seem to happen every day. Particularly with acquisitions and mergers, there must ultimately be a blend of one or more design functions. House styles may be quite different between the two or more companies, and almost inevitably, the role that design has traditionally played in each company is quite different.

Going back to our example, a very bright person founded a small company and led it to a point of growth that made it desirable for acquisition. The now-famous "offer you can't refuse" was made, and the founder found himself an employee of a larger firm. The founder also made a great deal of money with the transaction and was still "in charge," at least of his product line. Not wanting to give up everything, he wanted to put his own "stamp" on his division. The easiest way to do this is visually. (Anybody out there reading this ever run into a division head in a large company that wanted his or her own "look" for his division's materials?)

Sensing that the corporate house style was about to be forced on him, he quickly went to his old college chum who was a designer, and had him develop a whole set of materials. He also realized that once he had these materials produced, more than likely the parent corporation would let him keep them. After all, they had just spent a great deal of money to acquire his product line, and they certainly wanted a quick return on their investment. It was highly unlikely that the parent company would come down very hard on him over a few new logos and sales materials.

What the design manager should have done in this example was to call the new division head as soon as he was appointed, introduce himself, and then schedule an introductory meeting. Instead, the design manager waited until the new division head introduced materials that were not well designed or (according to house style rules) correctly designed. The design manager had missed a prime opportunity to establish a mutually valuable relationship with the new division head. When design managers wait until there is a perceived "design crisis" to confront a senior nondesign executive, then they are perceived as a "logo cop." Being perceived as the logo cop is very dangerous. It certainly doesn't help in your quest to be an equal, strategic business partner!

If the design manager had been proactive and met the new division head at the very beginning, it would have been much easier to develop a strategic business partner relationship in a totally nonthreatening, nonconfrontational way. The design manager should not go to such an initial meeting with a copy of the corporate design specs, wearing his or her logo cop badge like a dinner plate! Rather, the design manager should approach the new division head as an ally—a partner who offers to help in this transition using visual design elements, and an ally who is willing to listen first, then make creative suggestions as to how to assist the division head in meeting his or her business goals. This would have become a truly mutually valuable relationship.

When I was discussing ways to establish the role of design in business, I suggested a technique of using the organization chart to determine every function in the company and to determine how each function is dependent on design. I then suggested offering to go to staff meetings of each of these functions to explain how your design function could partner with the staff with respect to its specific needs for design. In a real sense, this is also the best way to develop mutually valuable relationships all across the company. As you visit each group, develop relationships with one or more individuals in that group who might become real supporters of design later on.

As I mentioned earlier, one of the strongest alliances I was able to leverage in my corporate career was with the law department. It seems that everything we do in design today has a legal perspective. Wouldn't it be better to have a mutually valuable relationship with the law department than to face the dreaded legal review?

Developing strong and healthy relationships is hard work—and it takes time. It requires tact, listening skills, and the ability to show genuine concern for the other party's needs—not just *your* needs. Above all, it means that a design manager who wants to become a strategic business partner, to be respected and trusted, and to become an important corporate asset rather than a "necessary evil," must take the initiative—and the time—to develop these kinds of relationships. Without *mutually* valuable relationships throughout the organization, you will never really be able to become a core, strategic partner. You will remain a service provider.

Implementing Efficient Work-With Processes

Please notice how this heading is phrased: "work-with." This is the opposite of "work-for." Recall my taxi driver analogy: we're talking about strategic partnerships, not simply providing a service. Instead of just driving the cab and telling your "customer" that you'll take them wherever they want to go, you must become a transportation consultant and offer advice on the best way to get there given their needs, time, and budget.

Working *with* someone is quite different from working *for* him or her. All too often, designers and design managers really do believe they are service providers rather than strategic business partners. Believe me, if in your head you think you are a service provider, that's exactly what everyone else will think too. But in addition to *thinking* you are a service provider, if you also *behave* like one, then that's all you and the design function will ever be in the corporate environment.

Nearly every design manager I have ever talked with uses the term "client" endlessly. Let's get it right. They are *partners*—not clients (or customers). Throughout my career, I made a very conscious effort never to think about people I worked with as clients, customers, or subordinates. The people who made up my staff were associates. The people we worked with on design projects were partners.

All of the stuff we have covered in the model so far is what makes this change possible. We have learned to understand and clearly articulate the true value of design to the enterprise in business terms. We have done exercises to fully appreciate and understand the role of design in the business, not as decoration, but rather as the visual manifestation of the core business strategy. We have proactively sought out key stakeholders in the company and developed mutually supportive, valuable relationships with them. Now is the time to truly be a partner, not a servant.

Learning to work with people, to be an effective collaborator and colleague, is easy for some people, but can be very difficult for many more. It requires an innate belief in your expertise, knowledge, and added value to a business. Unfortunately, we are never taught these things in design school. We learn how to be expert designers but not how to be trusted business colleagues. Just look around at the people who do this well. Lawyers, physicians, CEOs, marketing people, engineers, and nearly all other professionals realize they are necessary because of their expertise. Although under strict dictionary definitions they have clients, they don't behave like these people are their masters. They know the service they provide can often make the difference between the success and failure of a business or individual. The design profession has to get to the same place. An art service will never be truly valued in the business environment. However, people who make a significant and recognizable difference will be valued.

Should In-House Design Groups Charge a Fee for Design Work?

Whenever this discussion of working with people—rather than for them—comes up in my seminar, invariably participants raise the issue of in-house groups being required to charge a fee for their design work. Of course, the folks who work for an external agency must charge a fee for their time. This is how their agency makes money. But how about those internal groups?

Let me focus on the internal corporate design group first. If we agree that the goal is to become a strategic business partner in the corporation, a valued core competency, and a center for excellence, and to be sought out by every function in the business for advice and council about design issues, is that really realistic if we charge for that kind of service? I don't believe it is. Once we charge for our time, we go back to being a taxi driver, a provider of service for hire. If our nondesign colleagues in the company have to pay us for our assistance, why wouldn't it be all right for them to go outside of the company and pay the same fee to an external agency? After all, they probably think they can get what they "like" more easily from an outside firm that they are paying.

I really had to suffer with this problem with only one of my corporate positions. When I was hired by Digital Equipment Corporation to head up the corporate design unit of the company, I "inherited" about one hundred people in the group (which also included writers) and a charge-back system that had been in place since the company was founded. An hourly rate for each employee in my group had been established by the finance department. They had determined that, in my group (which they called a "cost center"), each employee had to bill back to other groups at least 68 percent of their available time each week. The figures had been determined by factoring in salaries, benefits, overhead for rent (occupancy charges in the headquarters), and all of the other costs associated with operating a design group (supplies, equipment, and so forth). This is more or less exactly how an external agency has to operate. I found myself running a boutique business inside of a larger business.

Each month I had to prepare complicated forecasts of revenue versus expense, then meet with two financial analysts to write a report on my "business." This would take several days of my time on a monthly basis. Internal "customers" would constantly remind me they could take their "business" elsewhere if I didn't give them exactly what they wanted in very short time frames. I realized immediately this system had to go away!

If I wanted to run my own agency, I would have done just that. I would have never joined a large corporation to spend about 80 percent of my time running a not-for-profit business. I wanted to make a contribution to the company as a design guru. I did not want to waste my valuable time concentrating on "making my numbers" each month.

My staff was, likewise, intimidated. They were afraid if they didn't bill out enough time each month, they might be laid off. As a result, they accepted all kinds of what was basically production work to ensure that they would have enough billable hours each month. They also had to keep cumbersome daily time sheets that I had to review on a weekly basis. The outcome of all this worry and record-keeping was less available time to develop really effective design solutions that would benefit the strategic goals of the company.

The process had been well established, and I knew that changing it would take some time and be met with a great deal of resistance, particularly from the finance people. However, I was determined to eliminate the system so that my group could get on with the critical work of doing strategic design for the company.

As part of the solution to this problem, I consulted with a number of my design management colleagues in other companies to determine how they had dealt with the problem. I talked with my friend John Tyson about this, since he had faced the same problem when he reset the design function at Northern Telecom. In the same article by Artemis March, she explained John's strategy this way:

Excerpt from "Paradoxical Leadership:
A Journey with John Tyson" by Artemis March

Tyson has committed his group to forging and continually renewing a "clear vision of how our product base is likely to change, and learning to be the first to identify the power shifts that will that will reshape [the] customers' definition of value." "Power shift" is a phrase heard frequently at CDG. Most simply, it means creating disjunctive shifts to future value.

Tyson understands that making a power shift is both an external and an internal process. He communicates his vision of it through distinct language and metaphor: "Metaphor is critical. It is a way to reach when other language becomes ineffective." His use of metaphor is aimed at getting people to switch paradigms, and to affect the internal power shifts that make external shifts possible, indeed, probable.

As Tyson explains it, changing the funding structure of CDG was an essential step in this process:

> We could not be going out with our tin cup. The funding must support the concept because the funding process creates the behavior. If you're a support function, then you shouldn't be surprised to find people selling or being in a reactive mode. Design Interpretive had been funded at the bottom—as subcontractors. So I challenged the organization from the standpoint of my accountability. The day we did the big reorganization, it was important that I stand up there and tell them I had attacked the issue of funding, and that we had reset it completely.

Later in the article, Tyson is quoted as follows:

But what happens if you are actually in control? What happens if, instead of going out with a tin cup or chasing golden doors, you go to the same meeting and you say, 'No, you don't understand. I'm not here to get money. I'm here to *invest* in your future'?

Tyson struck the words "client" and "selling" from the CDG vocabulary. Instead, he says, "Thou shalt use the word 'partner.'" Try lining that up with the tin cup! It doesn't. "Partner" lines up with "investment."

The bottom line is that if you are in a situation as an in-house group that must recover its costs by some kind of internal charge-back system, do everything in your power to eliminate that system. You will never be anything other than a service provider to the company as long as that system exists.

The method I used was to essentially follow my model. I created a presentation for senior management review that began with the *value of the design function to the bottom line of the business.* I gave very clear, businesslike examples of exactly what the role of design was in the business. I enumerated the benefits of mutually valuable, strategic relationships across all functions of the company. I described the numerous advantages of partnering with, rather than working for, key operating units. Finally, I had to prepare a detailed financial analysis and profile of how the new system would be accounted for in the financial reports of the corporation. I won. We became a single expense line on the corporate budget. I no longer had to spend an inordinate amount of time trying to figure out how to make money for my department. Rather, I was able to spend my time trying to figure out how to use design solutions to make money for the corporation.

External agencies have the same problem. It is very difficult for them not to be looked at as a service provider rather than a partner when they have to charge a fee for every hour spent creating effective design solutions. This simply means that the external agencies need to work very hard to minimize that perception. Think back to my comments about my personal physician. I do pay him a fee, but his expertise far outweighs the fee. Some courageous agencies have attacked this problem a little differently in the last few years. These agencies are quoting their fee based on the measurable results of the design work. If the outcome of their work shows a measurable financial gain for the company, then the agency gets a percentage of that gain as a fee. If the project fails, they get no fee at all.

A Global Example of Working with Partners

Let me provide you with one last real example of what working with partners is all about.

Clarence is the design manager for a U.S.-based company that has been expanding into the international marketplace over the past five years. Clarence's corporate design group, made up entirely of American designers, did nearly all of the company's design work. About the only design work not under the corporate group's control was the look and feel of the advertising, which was handled by a New York ad agency.

Company sales and marketing people based in Europe and Asia were expected to implement all design work created in the corporate headquarters without question. There were no trained designers on staff in the countries, and the U.S. ad agency's work was the only advertising they could run. From time to time, when sales and market share did not grow as planned in the countries, high-level meetings were held with the country managers. These country managers often pointed to the advertising, as well as the packaging design and the sales collateral materials, as being inappropriate for their countries.

Management looked at this as a weak excuse at best, but agreed to invite Clarence in to hear the country manager's complaints and other issues regarding design. They also invited the account manager from the advertising agency to attend the meeting. Both Clarence and the ad agency were convinced that their design work was excellent, strong, and compelling. Senior management agreed that there was probably nothing wrong with the design work, and were supportive of both Clarence and the ad agency.

As the day of the meeting approached, how would you have prepared yourself if you were Clarence? How would you have handled this situation?

Once again, I have selected an example that demonstrates a very common mistake by design managers and design groups. In this scenario, design was indeed valued by the CEO. The problem was that design was not valued by sales and marketing, particularly in various geographies. You need to be valued by *everyone*, not just the CEO.

Although the design work done by Clarence's group was apparently perceived to be working very well in North America, it was perceived as a core problem for effective sales and marketing outside of North America. Clarence was not working with, or partnering with, nondesign managers in the geographies and regions of this global company. Now it had led to one of those dreaded, confrontational, showdown meetings that none of us particularly enjoy. Clarence seemed ready to be defensive. Regional sales and marketing managers were preparing for war. This was not a healthy situation for anyone, and certainly not a healthy situation for the company and its sales growth or market share.

If Clarence had learned to be proactive and to work in partnership with these sales and marketing managers, the meeting would not even have be necessary. In fact, Clarence could have still made sure that the meeting never occurred.

His first step should have been to contact the managers in question and to *listen* to them with an open mind. Although some of these managers might have wanted to get into the largely subjective arena of aesthetics, Clarence needed to bring them back to the more objective areas of just why the design solutions his group had created were not effective in their geographies. Just what was not working? Why? He should have suggested partnering with them to find creative, effective solutions. Clarence also had to be prepared to admit that although his group's design work was very effective in North America, a European or Asian solution might be somewhat different. Then Clarence should have been prepared to find those design solutions that *would* work in various geographies.

This is what I call working with people. I am certain that the non–North American managers believed Clarence was nothing more than a decorative service provider who was not giving them the service they want. By being willing to listen to them and partner with them in finding effective design solutions, Clarence could have changed this dynamic dramatically. The real message here is to learn to work with *all* stakeholders rather than just pleasing any single audience, such as the CEO.

Of course, this relates directly to the design brief. In the audience section, the needs of *all* audiences—worldwide—must be articulated. In the business objectives/design strategy section, all geographical business objectives need to be listed, and each of those geographic objectives needs to have specific design strategies associated with it. The only way to be sure you are on the right track is to include representatives of various countries in your key stakeholder list and to be certain you consult with them through the whole design brief creation process.

In all circumstances—but particularly in global business situations—design managers need to make a concerted effort to investigate various audiences, and to learn how to develop effective design solutions to meet those various audiences' needs. I am a great advocate of design managers and individual designers attending such events as national and international sales meetings and trade shows. Even if the theme of these events does not seem to be directly related to design per se, they are opportunities for the design profession to learn more about key stakeholder needs and requirements firsthand.

The days of sitting in a design studio and "just doing" design are long over. The design profession must get out into the world and see what is going on. The design profession must actively listen to key internal stakeholders, as well as members of all of the various target audiences, in order to be able to create effective design solutions for these groups. You can't create brilliant design solutions by simply sitting in a cubicle somewhere. And it's very hard to work with and design for people you have never met, seen, or spoken to.

Credibility and Trust

Once you completely understand the added value you offer to any enterprise (personally and as a design function), once you understand

and effectively communicate the role of design in business, once you are able to develop mutually valuable relationships (emphasis on "mutually"), and once you develop the skills to work with people, not for them—then, and only then, will you begin to have real credibility as a strategic business partner.

Knowledge leads to understanding. Understanding leads to appreciation and credibility. Credibility leads to trust. First, people have to have some real knowledge and understanding of what added value design can offer. Only then will they begin to appreciate great design. Credibility stems from providing solutions that really work to meet the business objectives of the project. Once you have credibility, trust is inevitable.

Remember, as I have said time and time again, the core reason so many designers complain that they don't have enough time, don't have sufficient budgets, don't get invited into the process early enough, and aren't appreciated or understood, is because they aren't *trusted* as businesspeople in the first place. Don't forget that any enterprise, for-profit or nonprofit, is in existence solely to make money. A nonprofit business wouldn't be around very long unless it made enough money to pay the bills. A for-profit company, likewise, would disappear very quickly if it didn't make money.

In the minds of businesspeople, the purpose of design should first and foremost be to help meet these business objectives. It is up to the design profession to make them understand that this is our goal too. We need to let our business partners know that the purpose of design is far greater than just being "pretty" or "clever."

Nondesigners are nearly always the people who ultimately have final approval of design solutions. Think about that for a minute. People who really don't fully understand what they are approving and have no training or expertise in design end up as approvers of design! Why? Because designers are not trusted to make business evaluations. For the most part, most nondesigners *will* admit a professional designer knows more about the aesthetics of design than they do. They just don't trust designers to make the final evaluation of whether their design solution meets real business needs. In order for design to become an equal partner, a co-owner of projects, the design profession must first earn credibility and trust from its non-design partners. The model I have developed has already helped a great many design groups achieve this goal of credibility and trust. It certainly worked for me. Give it a try.

Chapter 8
Using the Design Brief in the Approval Process

This whole business of gaining approval for a design solution is among the most painful and frustrating processes design groups face on a routine basis. I certainly suffered through these approval meetings for a number of years early in my career in corporate design. Finally, I had to face the fact that I needed to find a way to take the pain, frustration, and suffering away. At first, I thought it might be a hopeless quest—the impossible dream, if you will. I recalled that in school, I had one graphic design professor who, at the time, I thought was particularly harsh with this approval process. Finally I realized that, in fact, he wasn't harsh at all—he was just preparing us for our careers!

He would assign a design problem for us to work through. On the appointed day when our solutions were to be presented, he would have us put our work along the ledge of the whiteboard in the classroom. Without saying a word, he would walk along the board and either leave your work where it was, or throw it on the floor!

Actually, almost everybody's work ended up on the floor. He would then turn to the class and say, "Everything on the floor fails. If you think your work hasn't failed, pick it up, put it back up on the ledge, and tell me and the class why it doesn't fail." Of course, most of us picked up our work and tried to defend it. After all, we didn't want to fail. While we desperately tried to defend our work, the professor kept interrupting by saying; "You're too proud and defensive of your clever design solution, put it back on the floor!"

What he was teaching us is that design should not be defended. Design should not be a success because *we* thought so. Rather, we only got to keep our work up on the ledge when we could clearly explain why our solution met the objectives of the assignment. For some reason, it took me a few years to really understand what this professor had taught us. It was always too easy in school to talk a lot about how clever (creative, etc.) we had been with an assignment. Other design students knew what we were talking about and were often very supportive. This is not the case in the corporate world. The other nondesign-trained stakeholders, particularly those who have the authority to approve—or disapprove—a design solution, are not cognizant of all the design techniques we know. They only know whether they like it or not.

The particular professor I am referring to was actually quite unique in his approach. What he was doing is certainly not the norm in most design classrooms today.

I have had the privilege of attending and speaking at a few *HOW Magazine* design conferences. At the HOW conferences, one evening is devoted to an event called "The Student Showcase." The conference organizers invite design school students who are in their last year of study to bring their portfolios and display their work for all of the conference attendees. I really look forward to this annual event. I am often amazed at the talent and ability displayed by these students.

I attended one of these Student Showcase events and spotted one student whose work was particularly impressive. The young man was a graphic design student and had a large display of posters and brochures he had designed. As I approached the table where he was presenting his portfolio, I overheard him explaining one of his brochures to an attendee of the conference. With a great deal of excitement and intensity, the young man explained that on the first spread he had introduced an emotional experience. On the next spread, he had enhanced this experience by adding bold colors and avant-garde typographic treatments. Finally, he explained, he combined all of these design elements to bring the brochure to an exciting, emotional climax!

What this student was doing was explaining the design techniques he had considered and used to create what he believed to be a visually stunning piece. To another designer, his work was indeed visually stunning. However, if he had used that kind of thinking in making a presentation of a brochure to a nondesign-trained CEO or marketing executive, he would have been in big trouble.

Let me assure you, I am not trying to belittle this student. He was doing what he was used to doing in design school. In design school, we present our work to fellow design students and design teachers. It seems normal to present design, well, as design. Unfortunately, this doesn't work in the corporate world. The people we will present design solutions to in the business world don't understand—or appreciate—the power of using negative space, bold color palettes, or unique typographic styles brilliantly. After we leave design school, we have to learn to present design solutions for final approval by nondesign business managers in an entirely new way.

The key is not to try to defend design solutions by talking about design elements, but to present the results of the design solution vis-à-vis the objective of the project. It is up to us, the designers, to point out why a particular design solution works to meet the stated business objectives. We take it away from the subjective and move it into the objective. The objective is found in the design brief, which then also becomes your approval presentation outline.

The Design Brief as an Outline for Approval Presentations

If you have carefully constructed a design brief as outlined earlier, then you have effectively created an outline for your approval presentation as well. I am talking about approval of a final design solution at this point, not various and sundry approvals throughout the course of the project.

Your presentation must begin with the very first paragraphs or bullet points in your design brief: the executive summary. You briefly review the key business elements: why we are doing this project, why we are doing it now, who we are doing it for, what business outcomes we expect, and so on. This sets up the facts that: 1) you thoroughly understand the project and the business needs clearly, 2) you understand the target audience(s), and 3) you worked strategically, in a highly businesslike manner.

Next, I would suggest moving straight through the brief as you constructed it, mentioning briefly who is ultimately accountable for the results (the co-owners) and who the key stakeholders are, and giving an overview of the various phases of the project. This should be followed by a description of the particular category (or categories) and its trends, the company portfolio (if applicable), certainly the target audience, and any other key elements that you may have included in your particular brief. If some of the items I have suggested in the general outline in chapter 3 have not been used, then leave them out!

When you get to the detail of the phases, be sure to clearly explain, in layman's terms, the content of the phase, why it was critical, who was involved, what, if any, approvals were made in the phase and by whom, and the results of any target audience testing that may have been done. The purpose of all of this is to make certain the approver understands there was a strategic, businesslike process followed and that key stakeholders were involved. The testing with target audience results demonstrates that your solution is not just the "decorative whim" of some artist!

Next, you show the approver one solution, and explain—clearly, in business terms—just why that solution meets all of the business objectives.

Finally, you describe the implementation of the project and the way in which you and your co-owner/partner will measure and report business results.

Understanding the Final Approver

People who have the authority and power to make final approvals of design solutions are human beings. Human beings all have unique personalities. Therefore, it behooves you and your co-owner/partner to find out as much as you can about the individual you will be presenting to. What motivates him? What basic needs does he have that frame his personality? Is he primarily motivated by power? Does he need to be clearly in control of everything, all of the time? If so, perhaps you need to keep this in mind as you prepare your presentation.

Other senior managers I have known are really more motivated by achievement. They are very proud of the things they have been able to accomplish in their careers. And they are usually very proud of the success their business has achieved so far. More than likely I would use a different style of presentation content for this type of individual. I would probably want to include something about how this represents yet another achievement for the company.

Finally, the most common type of personality I have run into in the ranks of very senior management are those people who are really driven by the need for affiliation. Down deep, they want to be loved by everyone—customers, employees, and shareholders. My style of presentation would be geared to this need differently than one I would prepare for a power person or an achievement-driven manager.

It is never enough to just create a one-size-fits-all presentation for approval of a design solution. Keep the audience for your presentation clearly in mind as you prepare for an approval meeting. It will help ensure a successful outcome to the meeting.

It is important to remember that very often the person (or persons) with final approval authority have not given this project one single thought until this very meeting. Usually they have not been involved throughout the design process, and therefore they need to be reminded, or told for the first time, what this project is all about in business terms. Do not talk about design! Talk about the *results* of the design project and how those results meet the business objectives. It is not necessary to rave on about your creative use of typography, color palettes, or other design elements. It is not necessary to invite subjective criticism. *Never* ask, "Do you like it?" (Invariably they won't!)

In my experience, it is also very dangerous to present more than one final design solution in a *final* approval meeting—even if there are two or three you know work equally well. If you present multiple design solutions, I can almost guarantee the approver will tell you that he or she "likes" certain elements of each solution you present and will ask, "Could you combine those various elements into one design?" What you will end up with is a hybrid solution that doesn't work. This approval process must not turn into a beauty contest. Design is a problem-solving discipline. Focus on the problem, and on how the single design solution you are presenting solves that business problem. Also, if you indicate there are two or three solutions that work equally well, you are simply signaling to the approver that you are not really sure which solution is the best. You are relinquishing ultimate accountability.

But what if, as many designers tell me is the case, the approver always insists that he or she wants to see at least two or three solutions? Ask yourself, Why is this the case? They want to see multiple solutions because they don't *trust you* to come up with a business-oriented solution on your own. They don't believe you know as much about the business need(s) as they do. They agree you can do design well, but they are the ones who will decide which design solution works best to solve the problem. This situation exists primarily because you have probably always presented design in design terms, not business terms. They are not used to hearing you talk about meeting business objectives.

To turn this situation around, you will initially have to be very careful in developing your presentation, and to be sure to mention the many concepts you explored—and tested—with the target audience. You should also be sure to mention that throughout the project, key stakeholders were actively involved, and that these stakeholders had agreed to the end result of each phase. This indicates to the approver that there were, in fact, multiple treatments considered, but this single one was the solution that best met the business criteria and objectives. If they still want to see other treatments, then simply say you will be back in a week or so to show them what had been considered, and explain why each of these early concepts had been rejected by the design team and by the key stakeholders. This is particularly effective if you have tested concepts with the target audiences and can indicate that your target business audience preferred the design solution you are presenting. In time, approvers will—hopefully—trust you more and be satisfied that you will only bring them design solutions for approval that really work in the marketplace to the benefit of the company.

If you absolutely must talk about certain design elements, don't do it until *after* you have made the business case for your design solution. Too many designers begin these approval presentations with lots of comments about specific design elements. This opens the door for the approver to jump in with highly personal and subjective comments. Always make the business case first.

Another critical aspect of creating an approval presentation is to be sure to include those last two phases I mentioned: implementation and measurement. By including these in your approval presentation, you will demonstrate your acceptance of accountability for the outcomes of the particular project. The approver will appreciate knowing a bit of detail about what will happen as the result of his or her approval and will definitely respond well to the fact that there are specific criteria in place to measure results in business terms.

Anticipating Objections

When you are preparing your approval presentation, think about your approver and what objections he or she is likely to raise. In print design, the two most common objections I encountered were: "Isn't the type awfully small?" and "Shouldn't the logo be larger?" Clearly there are many others that you could add from your own experience! The point is to anticipate these kinds of comments and to deal with them as you make your presentation in a way that will ensure the comments will never be made.

As an example, I remember presenting a design solution for a new corporate stationery system. This happened to be a very high priority for my CEO, and he was certainly one of those "Shouldn't the logo be larger, and the type be larger?" guys. A prime business objective of this project was to be sure that people in more than forty countries would all use the identical stationery system. Customers had been teasing the CEO about how his company "looked so different" in various parts of the world. He had taken this teasing very personally and was determined to solve the problem. This CEO was very driven by the need for affiliation. He desperately needed to be loved and appreciated by everyone. That is why this particular project was so critical to him. We understood this personality need of his and therefore created a presentation that would ease his mind. We were careful to note that a solution had been found that would satisfy, and *delight*, customers worldwide.

In order to address his anticipated comments about type size and logo size, we created our final approval presentation for the single system we had developed, tested, and were recommending, taking extra care to mention to the CEO that part of solving the problem was to accommodate often-lengthy addresses, postal codes, telephone information, and so forth, worldwide. We also pointed out that one reason various countries had developed their own unique stationery systems was that the amount of information required either by law or by standard regional business practice was quite different from the U.S. standard. Names and titles were often much longer. Some countries required business registration numbers to be included on all business papers. In most countries that used both their native language and English, both sides of the business card or calling card were used. Also, both languages might appear on the same page of a letterhead or other business form.

If the prime business objective was to create a single system that could be used globally, then that system had to be able to accommodate all of this diverse information as well as all of the various specific country needs. We went on to explain that the maximum amount of information, along with the standard sizes of business papers in each country, were used as two of many guidelines to determine the most workable and effective size of the type on the business papers, as well as the placement and size of the company logo. We also explained that our solution had been tested and deemed successful by representatives of the target audience in each geographical region.

Now, this may seem like a lot of extra effort in an approval presentation, but it accomplished our goal. How could the CEO say the type was too small, or the logo was too small, after we had carefully explained a process that had led us to a solution that ultimately met the prime business objective? We had anticipated some of his comments and objections and effectively dealt with them in our presentation. He never raised the issue. If he *had* still asked if the type couldn't be larger, we would have answered by reiterating our process, and focusing a bit more on how well the solution had been received by various country managers when we asked them to review it with their customers. I would never get into a debate over the size of the type, or the use of specific font in an approval presentation, particularly with a CEO. I know I would lose. The trick is to use rational, businesslike discourse in an approval presentation, to not dwell on the relative merits of some design element, and to anticipate possible negative or subjective comments from the approver. Again, explain why it *works*, not why it is pretty.

What If You Can't Make the Presentation Yourself?

In some companies, unfortunately, the designer or design manager has not traditionally been allowed to present his or her own design solutions to the final approver. Someone else decides that he will do it for you!

There are a number of ways to deal with this. In the beginning, before you have reached that point where you have credibility and trust as a strategic design manager, you might have to accept this obstacle. The best thing to do in these situations is to create the type of presentation I have been discussing anyway and give it to the individual who is scheduled to present for you. A couple of things could happen at this point. The person might simply say "Thank you" and go off and do the presentation alone. In this case, at least the person has a bulletproof set of materials to use. After all, you created the presentation! A better scenario would be for the person to say, "You really ought to come with me." And, of course, the very best result is that the person would say, "You do this so well, why don't you come with me, and make the presentation yourself?"

Over time, your ultimate goal is to always be the one who makes design solution presentations for approval. The concept of having co-owners in developing the brief, who are equal partners and equally accountable, should also help you in making the argument that approval presentations must be made by those who are *accountable* at the end of the day. It takes time to change company cultures and traditions. Don't panic if you find it will be necessary to slowly migrate to a new tradition of design always being presented by design professionals. The key is that you are moving forward, not simply accepting the status quo as a *fait accompli*.

What If You Are Just Not Comfortable Making Presentations to Senior Managers?

I know many talented designers and design managers who just cannot stand up in front of a group, or even a single senior manager, and make an effective presentation. For some of these people, a solution is to take some courses or get some coaching on effective public speaking. For others, it might be hopeless. They just aren't comfortable in these situations, and it shows. For this latter case, I would suggest enlisting the aid of your co-owner, nondesign business partner to stand up and make the presentation. It doesn't mean you can't develop the presentation, it just means that it is important to present the design solution in the most effective, compelling way, and that might mean getting some help from your partner. However, you still must be present at the presentation. To not show up would signal that you are really not accountable for your design solution.

A Final Word on Approvals

This may startle you, but a mentor of mine, early in my career, once said to me, "Never ask for approval, simply thank the approver for it!" I must admit, I was pretty skeptical about this approach at first. I had not yet reached the point where I was completely trusted and had the kind of credibility that would allow me to be so brash, especially in the presence of the CEO! At first I waffled a bit and said things to the CEO like, "I'm sure you will agree with us that this is the best design solution for our business objectives." I was equally startled to find out that this tactic actually worked! Once I reached that point, I never went back. I never again said, "We *hope* you will approve." Much later, I was actually able to say, "We appreciate your approval." My mentor told me, "When you ask for approval, or worse, *hope* for approval, you signal that the other person knows better than you do whether your design solution actually works. If you know it works, stand up for it. Explain why it works in business terms that the approver can understand."

Chapter 9
What Is a Design Manager?

Throughout this book, I have referred to both designers and design managers. Assuming we all know what a designer is, I'd like to focus on the term *design management*.

For most of my career, I encountered puzzled looks when I would answer the question, "And what do you do?" by saying, "I am a design manager." The usual response was, "What on earth is that?" For those of you who are design managers, or who aspire to become one, it seems essential that we figure out an understandable response to the question, "Just what is a design manager?"

In my seminar, "Managing Design for Strategic Advantage," I ask participants to explain what a design manager is. Invariably, there are as many answers as there are participants. Design managers often have a difficult time explaining their role in an enterprise, even to other design managers! Is it any wonder that nondesign business managers don't understand our role either? If we truly want to become a core, strategic business partner, then we must learn to clearly articulate our particular role in the business.

Earl N. Powell, former president of the Design Management Institute, tackled this issue in an article entitled "Developing a Framework for Design Management"[1] in the *Design Management Journal*. Earl clearly and succinctly expressed not only my beliefs but also the beliefs of many other design managers in this article. In fact, I decided to use this article in my seminar as "pre-work reading" for participants. With Earl's permission, I am including the full text of the article here.

Excerpt from Design Management Journal, *by Earl Powell*

Developing a Framework for Design Management

Since the early eighties, when I was a practicing design manager, I have often thought about how best to describe what it is I do. How does one define design management, understand its objectives, and establish a framework for the knowledge, skills, and attitudes essential to its success? Writing this article has given me an opportunity to sort through the bits and pieces strewn about my office, and to recollect discussions I've had during almost twenty years of design management.

We've talked about the title itself—is it design management, or is it managing design? We've considered the context in which it happens, whether that is fashion design, machine-tool design, or graphic design. I've participated in endless discussions of the role of the design manager as design group manager, or as individual designer managing a design project. Lately, there's been considerable attention paid to the objectives and benefit of the design manager as a partner or key player in the evolving vision and strategy of an organization—and to design working as a competitive weapon.

Over the past ten years, the Design Management Institute has done design management research, developed education materials, provided education conferences and seminars, and developed publications to encourage design managers to become leaders in their professions and to help nondesign managers understand the importance of design for business success. All of these initiatives serve the ultimate goal of design and its management: to improve the quality of our lives by improving our experiences with our material world.

Recently, in a discussion with some design managers and educators in London, I realized that the Institute is doing all of this work to facilitate managing for design—a process of visual reasoning and decision making. This profession that we are striving to understand, develop, and support manages and shapes the context in which design can be most effective. And there are two sides to achieving this: First, the greater context—the organization itself—must be aware of the power of design for competitive advantage; and second, the professional responsible for the design group must be a leader with a core set of knowledge, skills, and attitudes.

I remember a meeting in the late eighties of the Institute's board of directors and board advisors (now called the "advisory council"), in which we attempted to agree on a definition for design management. I stress "attempted" because it is very hard to agree on a comprehensive definition of most important concepts without first establishing the context in which it applies. The definition we agreed on and which we believe could be applied to most situations was: *"the development, organization, planning, and control of resources for the user-centered aspects of effective products, communications, and environments."*

This definition does not work perfectly for all contexts, nor does it achieve much specificity. However, it does provide a general outline of the domain of design management.

As the world we experience becomes more complex and changing, the variety of our encounters with products and services increases and becomes more complicated. These encounters and experiences shape our thinking patterns, our behaviors, and even our language. Every encounter we have, whether it's seeing and smelling a flower, or filling a cup with freshly brewed coffee, begins with perception. The primary goal of design is to shape perceptions and therefore experiences of products and services. Thus, the goal of design management is to ensure that an organization uses a design resource effectively to achieve its objectives.

One of the key challenges businesses have faced in the last decade has been to get "close to the customer." Those that have succeeded in meeting this imperative have charged design with the responsibility of shaping perceptions of the organization itself, as well as its products and services. As the pace of change accelerates, design managers are further challenged to learn more about managing their groups, and about operating the enterprise.

Outlining precisely the knowledge, skills, and attitudes that provide an effective platform for the design manager to succeed depends equally on the context in which those skills are to be used. However, for both the corporation and the consultant design manager, managing for design means creating a context in which design can fully participate in all decisions that will shape the points of contact with, or the perceptions of, customers.

In my opinion, there are six categories of knowledge, skills, and attitudes that make up an essential core for the successful manager of design. These six areas overlap and share many qualities; they are only keys to rich domains of information and requisite actions. Three of them are intangible, qualitative, and softer; the other group tends to be pragmatic, tangible, and more measurable. The first group includes *purpose, people,* and *presence*; the second includes *process, project,* and *practice.* And each of these categories has its champions and its chroniclers, some of which I'll list in the following pages.

Purpose: *Purpose is the fuel of life, giving both energy and direction.*
For good reason, we always admire an individual or an organization with a clear sense of purpose. Their purpose gives them an energy and output that keeps them ahead of the pack. They seem to have most of the answers first; momentum propels them forward. Purpose appears frequently in discussions about leadership.

The design manager needs to have a clear sense of individual purpose. As well, this person must shape the purpose of the group he or she is managing, and ensure that this purpose meshes with that of the organization. Such a manager is valuable to the organization and prized by his or her group. When employees move from routine performance in completing their assignments to stellar performance that goes beyond those assignments, they have moved from being managed to being led. Sound management is the bedrock of leadership, as well as crucial to any effective organization.

There is an old saying, "If you don't know where you're going, you won't know when you get there." I would add that without purpose, you won't know where, when, or how to start. Also, I would say that the design manager must be vigilant to ensure that all of his or her decisions work toward a chosen purpose. The design manager who aims the group toward achieving the highest possible levels of product function, without an equal emphasis on product appearance, may find the company's products lose market share to those with equal function and superior appearance. Similarly, a shift in emphasis toward function can easily occur on a development project that simply demands extra attention to function.

In any organization, there are many dimensions and layers of purpose, and each may respond to different sources. Sometimes, decisions are made as a result of internal politics rather than customer needs. The design manager needs to create a context in which purpose is dedicated to keeping development processes focused, efficient, and effective.

Kenneth R. Andrews's book, *The Concept of Corporate Strategy*[2] is a classic work that sees good management in terms of three key components. First, as an organization leader, the manager builds the infrastructure and processes that give a group of individuals an effective operating capacity. Second, the manager's leadership role is won through effective communication, respect, attitude, and vision. Third, as architect of group purpose, the manager shapes and continually enhances the direction, strategy, and purpose of the group. Andrews's book belongs in every design manager's library.

People: *People are the building blocks of organizations. Their actions and decisions determine their future.*
The design manager's capacity to focus and motivate creativity is essential for effective results. He or she must continually clarify expectations by example and by the use of

careful communications to bring the best efforts to the right task at the right time. Design managers need to be able to understand and empathize with their designers' individual talents, and match them with the needs of the organization. They must also continually build and reinforce the core values and capabilities of the group and its position in the organization.

As design managers nurture creative capacity within their own groups, they can benefit the organization as a whole by helping nondesign managers learn how to to facilitate creativity in their groups and in development teams. For example, one key to creative thinking is reserving judgment in the early development stages and allowing all ideas to be considered. Once nondesign managers learn how effective this method is, they can set an example for their own groups. Thus the design manager can have a ripple effect throughout the organization.

Professor James Adams, who has written for the *Design Management Journal* and is a frequent speaker at DMI's education conferences, is the author of *Conceptual Blockbusting*[3] This book describes several blocks to creativity and offers strategies for dealing with them. Another helpful read is Jay Conger's *Winning 'Em Over: A New Model for Managing in the Age of Persuasion.*[4]

Presence: *The unwritten dimensions of an organization that operate informally, yet have a powerful influence on decisions and human interactions.*

There is a fundamental human need for stability, consistency, and meaning, and organizations are more effective when these traits are present. The culture of an organization forms to meet this need and is a process of establishing shared basic assumptions that are brought to bear on all decisions. Managers refer to this as the informal process of the organization. Often heard of as "the company way," this corporate culture consists of tacit knowledge and the acceptance of the organization's values and norms.

Understanding this corporate presence can reveal to the design manager key points for facilitating change, as well as formidable barriers to change. This is particularly important in attempting to infuse the organization with an attitude that respects and values design. Legend has it, for example, that during the early days of Apple Computer, Steve Jobs continually challenged his people to "make their computers insanely great for the individual." This became a shared value, an underlying assumption of the organization, and it helped to produce Apple's user-friendly products.

Dr. Edgar H. Schein's book, *Organizational Culture and Leadership*[5] provides a clear explanation and analysis of corporate culture, along with some excellent examples.

Process: *The complex process of moving from concept to market demands careful thought and broad expertise.*
Design is the only discipline that has the process of idea development at the core of its education program and practice. No other discipline focuses as deeply or broadly on the creation and evolution of ideas. The capacity of designers to take an idea through a development process, examining the evolving concept all along the way from multiple viewpoints, is unique and part of the design manager's contribution to organizational success.

Peter Keen's excellent book, *The Process Edge,*[6] is written from a business perspective, but embraces many concepts of process used by designers in their daily work and thought. This book is essential if you want to understand the power of process for business success or to expand your own understanding of process.

Project: *Managing or working on a project team is much more than just meeting schedules.*
Here is where we learn about the norms and values of our organizations, where professional development occurs, and where most of the political battles are fought. Taking charge of or being a member of a project team on the one hand challenges the people skills of the design manager; on the other, it fits well with his or her skills of viewing problems from multiple viewpoints and solving them through the development process. These skills are fundamental and unique to a designer's education. Design managers need to help the members of their groups utilize this capacity in order to take on leadership roles on their respective project teams.

Managing Projects and Programs, a collection of related articles from the *Harvard Business Review,* provides a good reference on project management. Also, *Project Leadership*[7] by Briner, Geddes, and Hastings provides insight into project leadership, teams, and project stage management.

Practice: *Practice supports the design resource group through the day-to-day operations of finance, performance planning, and human resource development.*
Achieving a balance of all aspects of design management is important and making sure the practice issues are given sufficient attention is a particular challenge. I see practice as a kind of platform to support the design group. I can remember that as an artist I really preferred painting over doing inventory, stretching canvas, sending bills to the gallery, and all those other things that were

the practical side of being an artist. Later, as a design manager, because I strongly believe in continuous learning and professional development, I remember attending budgeting meetings and fighting for as large a professional development budget as possible for my group. I didn't particularly enjoy the budgeting and financial side of design management, but it was great to give my group opportunities to develop professionally. Learning the concepts of budgeting and finance is important. For a basic understanding of finance, I recommend the self-directed course in *Essentials of Accounting*,[8] by Robert N. Anthony.

Another important aspect of practice is holding effective meetings. William R. Daniels's *Group Power II: A Manager's Guide to Conducting Regular Meetings*[9] is excellent and points out many subtle but powerful issues surrounding effective meeting practices.

In the end, good practice by the design manager becomes transparent, or is simply there supporting the group without being noticed.

Bringing It All Together

If you were enrolled in a formal degree program in management, you would probably find a few differences from what I have mapped out here. For example, read "strategy" for "purpose," "culture" for "presence," and "operations management" for "practice." To me, the simplicity of these words goes straight to the heart of things. But no matter what we call these skills, I believe they provide the fundamental framework for managing for design. How you adapt this framework for managing to your unique set of experiences, and how they continue to contribute to this framework, are important to me and to the profession of design management.

How the Most Successful Design Managers Describe Design Management

Fortunately, over the years I have been able to develop a rather extensive network of colleagues in design management. A large part of this network was developed through more than thirty years of participation in the Design Management Institute. Others in my network I have met through both my corporate and consulting activities. Many of these people were asked to present their views in an article also published in the *Design Management Journal*.[10] Here are just a few relevant quotes from some of these managers.

> Design management articulates simple explicit and implicit communications that mirror the organization's values. It nurtures individual contributions that accurately express and interpret the organization's business objectives. Design management is not a departmental or a supervisory role. It is a strategic resource and purposeful organizing process. Organizations that integrate design management as a continuously reformative activity within their culture easily survive competitive challenges and the subtle cultural and technological changes that cripple reactive organizations.
>
> —Tim Bachman, Principal, Bachman Design Group

> As a profession, design management strives to initiate and handle design strategies in boardroom decisions and to follow up with implementation and communication. Design management strives to create understanding and awareness among personnel at all levels that conscious actions in even the smallest decisions are the core of design management. Design management functions in all places and situations in which the organization, through its structure, products, and employees, makes decisions about customer experiences and product quality.
>
> —Torsten Dahlin, President, Swedish Industrial Design Foundation

Design is the ultimate vehicle to communicate intent. Penultimate design is the execution of leadership vision. I manage design strategically and tactically as a pure and essential element that supports our vision, which is in turn built upon our strategic plan. If the strategic plan changes, then our design work has to change along with the vision. The vision drives our design work. Design can crystallize senior management's thoughts and can help them move from the conceptual to the real world of implementation. I think that design management is visionary leadership.

—Lizbeth Dobbins, Manager of Corporate Branding and Identity, United States Postal Service

Effective design managers are linked with strategic marketing, as well as with engineering. Effective design management produces compelling value—tangible and intangible—for the company, and the company knows it. Effective design management contributes to the development of customer profiles and value propositions that drive commercialization as information that is translated into product form, color, texture, and interaction style. Excellent design practices influence corporate identity, affect day-to-day operations, and are consistent with the strategic goals of an organization. Expanding design management/leadership roles and extolling the value of design to the company are the subject of constant scrutiny internally, and a source of very stimulating conversations certainly. Are we there yet? Not necessarily. Is there progress? Absolutely."

—Patrick Fricke, Manager of Graphic and Visual Interface Design, Design Resource Center, Eastman Kodak Company

Design management can enhance the strategic goals of an organization through vision leadership—that is, with the help of 2D and 3D materials—thus providing a reflection of the organization's aspirations. Day-to-day operations can be enhanced through effective participation in the activities that give substance to those aspirations. Ultimately, the identity of the organization will be a function of the balance between the visionary and the practical. Design management, in particular, is well suited to help strike such a balance.

—Martin Gierke, Brand Research & Education Manager, Global Brand Management Group, Caterpillar, Inc.

Design, from an etymological perspective, means 'scribing'— a gesture about how an organization expresses its ideology, culture, products, and services. These assets are carefully guided so that the message is consistent and clear in all forms of expression. This coherency of message builds strength in the facilitation of strategic organizational functions, such as marketing, sales, and operations. Although the word 'management' creates decidedly tactical associations, what most organizations crave is 'leadership,' which is the necessary complement to management. Leadership is inherently inspirational—defining the vision and pointing in the direction of possibilities.

—Tim Girvin, Principal, Tim Girvin Design, Inc.

Most organizations share a common goal: to be perceived as better than and different from their competitors. Design management could be described as visual perception management. It contributes to realizing strategic goals if it ensures that the organization's visual language is consistent, distinct, and relevant for all its internal and external stakeholders. Design management is responsible for the design, implementation, maintenance, and constant evaluation of all items that are part of the total brand experience, from the instruction leaflet to the serviceman's uniform. For perception to become reality, design management needs to be one of its creators.

—Fennemiek Gommer, Partner, SCAN Management Consultants

In ideal terms, design management is a holistic, long-term activity, encompassing all levels of corporate functions. In long-term relationships, products, communications, environments, and services can be treated as a system. We use the concepts of 'bridge' and 'network' to express this sense of connectivity in all its strategic power—that is, design functions across all corporate activities, as well as projects from start to finish. Embedding design in all development processes on a day-to-day basis helps companies evolve in response to new opportunities and unforeseen conditions in unstable markets.

—Tetsuyuki Hirano, President, Hirano & Associates Inc.

As companies have come to recognize the enormous power their visual representation possesses to communicate, motivate, and inspire, design management has become asset management. Effective asset management reduces costs and builds value. Implementing systems that ensure a company is consistently represented over time decreases marketing costs as impressions build on one another to create image quality. Beyond asset management, design management is about attitude management. It represents not just a company's state of affairs, but its state of mind as well. As a company struggles to differentiate itself in the marketplace, its attitude is often the only critical difference between it and its competitors. Warm, friendly, professional, edgy—each evokes an emotion that can be visually portrayed. Good design management understands an organization's personality and communicates its attributes. At its best, design management is design leadership. It respects the past while guiding the present with an openness to the future.

—Tim Larsen, President, Larsen Design + Interactive

Design management is defined principally from a business and customer context, and it starts with a well-defined value proposition that is strategic to the client, followed by clear statements of vision, mission, goals, strategies, and action plans that link to those of the client and its business. Design management is about ensuring that the energy of the organization is expended in programs that ere essential and strategic. This is achieved when linkages between goals, strategies, plans, and processes have been clearly established and shared by design management. As a result, all employees in the organization can see the alignment of their work with high-level strategic priorities. Fundamental to achieving this level of organization and management maturity is the adoption of a management/leadership system spanning a wide range of elements, including organizational values, performance expectations, communications, and focus on external and internal customers, as well as constant monitoring of overall results. If the value proposition of the design organization is strongly associated with renewal, reinvention, and out-of-the-box thinking, it is essential that design management be active in the executive forums responsible for giving direction and determining investment in advanced product research.

—Peter Trussler, Vice President,
Corporate Design Group, Nortel.

Design is critical to achieving corporate mission. This means using design to help provide customers with what they want in a way that adds value to our business. In practical terms, we do this by defining what customers and other stakeholders want, and then developing the mechanisms for delivering it.

—Raymond Turner, Group Design Director, BAA PLC

Well, there you have it. Leading design managers from every corner of the globe responding to the question, What is the definition of design management?

As you can see, these leading practitioners of design management can rarely agree on a specific definition. However, every one of them agrees that design management is a core part of corporate vision, business strategy, and competitive advantage. It is far more than "project management," or simply providing administrative leadership to a corporate function. It requires a thorough understanding of the company's business strategy, the state of the industry on an ongoing basis, knowing the customer as well as anyone in the company, and understanding how to make the company's products or services leaders in the category through visual means. Great design managers also know how to translate all of this to their design staffs in a clear and meaningful way.

It is also interesting to note that they all agree that design management is more about the *results* of design and the *outcomes* of design than it is about the *aesthetics* of design. The most successful design managers always hire the best design talent they can find. If you do this, it is not really necessary to see your role as a teacher of design to design staffs. Rather, it is to be sure these excellent designers clearly understand the problem to be solved, as well as the desired outcomes of the design project.

The design brief process outlined in this book is the most effective way for the design manager to organize thinking, then communicate it to design staffs, as well as to the rest of the company. Review the critical elements of the design brief I outlined in chapter 3, and then reread these design manager's comments. You will see that they would all agree that these core elements are the basis of a complete understanding of the problem to be solved, which in turn leads to a comprehensive design strategy for a project vis-à-vis the business objectives.

I would also encourage you to apply these comments to my model. Each of the design managers I quoted referred to the importance of a value statement for design, understanding the role of design in the business, developing powerful mutually valuable relationships across all functions of the company, and working with people effectively.

If you are struggling with your value statement at this point, I encourage you to look at the comments in these various quotes. They are loaded with thoughts about what the real value of design is to any enterprise.

Finally, these people are leaders in the design profession simply because they understand how to articulate the value of design and they know how to think strategically in a business environment.

So, What's My Answer to the Question, "What Do You Do?"

Earl Powell gives us some excellent food for thought about what design management should be all about. He has also provided some handy references to books that may be of help to designers or design managers who are aspiring to make design a core, strategic business component of any company.

Although I used a lot of variations, my standard answer to people who asked me what a design manager did was something like: "I am a strategic business partner in my company and a key player in shaping the vision and business strategy of the company by making the company and its products (or services) visible through design."

I also often said, "I am accountable for the visual manifestation of the company's business strategy as approved by the board of directors and ratified by the shareholders." That used to draw some attention! In one instance I made that statement to the CEO of a company. He asked me to have lunch and discuss all of this further. We became good friends, and I started to get invited to meetings he called to discuss business strategy.

Chapter 10
Measuring Design Results

This whole question of how to measure design results has plagued designers for years. In every seminar session I have taught, participants raise this issue, usually saying, "My company always wants to know how we knew if our design work was successful or not. They want to see dollar figures that prove there was a return on the investment. There is no way to do that."

It is my belief that the cause of this dilemma is that designers, as well as nondesign business partners, are still focusing on aesthetics, or beauty. Of course, you can't qualitatively measure something that subjective. Beauty is still largely in the eye of the beholder. In fact, the stalemate that stems from this focus on aesthetics is one of the main reasons design functions are looked at as a "necessary evil."

At the end of the day, the only way to measure design is to measure whether the design solution met the business objectives and delivered the desired outcomes of the project. And those objectives should have been very clearly articulated in the design brief.

I recently saw a cartoon in the newspaper in which the design manager of a company said, "Look at this design award we just won for this brochure." The business manager says, "But the product isn't selling, and the competition is cleaning our clock!" The design manager retorts, "Who do you want to believe, the design experts who gave us an award for design excellence, or customers who don't appreciate great design?"

Good Design versus Effective Design

Just because design is technically great doesn't necessarily mean it is *effective* design in terms of the desired business objectives and business outcomes, especially in a corporate environment. Design awards are great—if they are legitimate awards—but they shouldn't be the only way you measure design.

I know of a product (which I am not at liberty to name) that is in every way a prime example of great industrial design. In fact, this product is on permanent display in a world-class museum. This product is also discussed in several textbooks on product design. Quite frankly, it is a brilliant example of stellar design technique. It has certainly won many design awards. So, what's the problem? The product didn't sell. The target audience didn't want it. Sure, it was beautiful, but not really very practical in the minds of the target audience. This particular product cost nearly a million dollars to develop. So, while those of us in the design profession can marvel at its beauty, functionality, and elegance, the senior nondesign business management of the company looked at this product as a waste of time and money. From management's point of view, it was good design—maybe they would even admit it was great design—but from their perspective it was a very costly mistake. In fact, they considered firing the lead designer on the project. (They didn't.)

The lesson to be learned from this example is that, as I have said repeatedly, to be truly valued in the corporate world, design must not only be great, but it also needs to solve the stated business problem and meet the business objectives. The only way nondesign business managers will accept the design profession as a core, strategic business partner is when they see that designers and design managers also value measurable business outcomes.

This doesn't mean we shouldn't be striving to create the very best design solutions possible. This doesn't mean that design shouldn't be exciting and elegant. This simply means that we must pay attention to assuring these fabulous design solutions also solve the stated business problem.

Some kinds of design are somewhat easier to measure in business terms than others. Product design is perhaps the easiest to quantify in business terms because it will be quickly apparent if the product sells or not. Packaging design can also be measured by some of the same criteria. Did the package "leap off the shelf into consumers' shopping carts"? Of course, sales, marketing, and advertising professionals will also claim the product was a success because of their efforts. But designers shouldn't be timid. They need to claim their role in a product's success. How do you prove this? By testing with the target audience. I can't repeat it often enough: Design solutions *must* be tested with the target audience. The results of these tests will give you a firm foundation for your claims of a design's effectiveness. Advertising agencies do this as a matter of course. They have all kinds of data to support their claims about advertising effectiveness. They always talk about reach, frequency, audience test results, and recall. Designers need to learn to do the same thing.

Graphic design is, admittedly, harder to quantify in business terms. How do you know a brochure, poster, or catalog, contributed to—or detracted from—making a sale? Once again, it has to be measured by returning to the original business objectives, and accompanying design strategy, from the design brief. Did the design strategy you used meet the business objective? If it did, the design was effective. If it didn't, the design solution did not work. It doesn't mean the design per se wasn't good; it simply means that the approach, the design strategy, didn't accomplish the stated goals.

Previously I gave an example of a stationery system for a company. The primary goals included ensuring that every operating unit of the company worldwide would be able to use the exact same stationery system. This was deemed critical by the CEO to ensure that customers would never be confused about what company they were dealing with. The measurement? A single global system was designed, tested worldwide with the target audience, and implemented. Customers stopped complaining that they were confused. Therefore, the design solution worked from a business perspective. Whether it won a design award or not, if it hadn't been accepted and implemented worldwide, then it wouldn't have met the business objectives of the project. Of course, it also must be good design. You must always strive to deliver great design—that works.

Shortly after implementing the new stationery system worldwide, I got an unpleasant phone call from a salesperson. This particular individual proceeded to tell me everything that was wrong with our design solution and that "customers hate it!" I told the salesperson that this was important input. I asked if he could give me the names of the customers who had told him how much they hated our new design. I told him I would like to speak with them personally to find out what was not working. Of course, the salesperson could not give me any names. I then offered to send him a list of all the customers worldwide that had been part of our test group and loved our solution. The salesperson just hung up on me, and I never heard from him again. The moral of this story is that you need to be careful with people who want to offer their own entirely subjective opinions about what they personally like or don't like in design. The only effective way to respond to these folks is to be armed with target audience test results.

Value Measured in Dollars

Was it worth the financial investment? It was if the project came in near or under the approved budget, and if the end result was deemed important enough for this investment. Once again, this all comes from the design brief process. Remember, the initial discussion on a design brief includes: Why are we doing this? Why are we doing it now? Why is it worth the time? How much money is allocated? Later, in the phase description process, the co-owners should discuss (debate) the time allocated to each phase, and the budget for the phase. Once the co-owners and the team of key stakeholders have agreed to all of this, then, and only then, should design work begin. And there is your measurement! Did we meet the business objectives in time and under the budget agreed to? Did the target audience respond in the manner we desired? Measuring success of a design project is really that clear-cut. The discussion should never revolve around "Was it pretty?" There is no way to effectively measure that in business terms.

Measurement Phase

By including a phase at the end of the design brief that outlines just how you plan to measure results, and what criteria will be used for that measurement, you move away from all that subjective nonsense after the fact, wherein people offer personal opinions about your design. Personal reactions are okay for "art," not for design.

Chapter 11
Strategies for Creating a Strong Intellectual Property Position
Joshua L. Cohen

Though a strong intellectual property position is often critical to a design's success in the marketplace, it is too often left as an afterthought. So are there benefits of considering intellectual property strategies from the very beginning of the design project? What are the risks of failing to do so? If IP strategies are to be considered from the beginning how can they be integrated into the design process itself?

Design briefs provide the first and best opportunity to set a design project on the right path. They help ensure that the resulting design meets the design manager's vision, embodies the core creative concept, and satisfies key criteria for advancing business objectives. A strong IP position is one of those key criteria.

Best outcomes result when IP is considered from the outset of a design project and when a roadmap for a strong IP position is specified in the design brief. When considered from the outset, a strong IP position can become an organic byproduct of every design project, resulting in a truly "ownable" design that enjoys comprehensive IP protection while respecting IP rights of others. This chapter explains the meaning and benefits of design ownership and introduces—in the context of design briefs—best practices for securing and sustaining strong IP positions by integrating design and legal strategies.

The Concept of "Design Ownership"

Firms face a growing imperative to offer unique products, protect that uniqueness, and sustain the competitive advantage it confers.[1] Put simply, an important objective of design managers is to produce designs that stand out in the marketplace.[2] In fact, design managers are now expected to deliver designs that stand out and give consumers a reason to choose them over competitive offerings, thus creating an enviable distance between their product offering and that of their competitors.

IP-savvy design managers aspire to develop products that will be superior to existing products, that will not infringe the IP rights of others, and that will enjoy the valuable competitive advantages conferred by IP protection. By recognizing the importance of a strong IP position to commercial success, companies are poised to pursue design ownership—the enviable position of being both armed with IP rights to exclude others from adopting their unique design and free to use that design while respecting the IP rights of others.[3]

From the IP perspective, therefore, the ideal design is one that can be "owned" in that it is both protectable by IP rights (to establish a sustained competitive advantage) and free of others' IP rights (to reduce the risk and uncertainty associated with potential conflict and litigation).

Such design ownership can and should be made a deliverable of every design project. In other words, it should be made an organic byproduct of the design project as defined in the design brief. Doing so is what makes a design successful from the IP perspective.

Pursuing a Design Protected by IP Rights

To achieve a design that is protected by IP rights, design management must first decide just how the design should best stand out in the marketplace. The selected strategy is then set forth in the design brief itself, together with a roadmap for planned comprehensive IP protection.

Specifying Uniqueness in the Design Brief

To establish a strong IP position, design managers should at the outset consider how elements of a design should differentiate it from competitive offerings. Design managers should specifically consider whether differentiation is achieved in terms of functional elements (e.g., performance, cost, longevity, efficacy); in terms of elements of form (e.g., aesthetic appeal, brand and source identity); or both.

Is the decision to purchase a prospective product offering in a targeted product category driven by aesthetic appeal? Or perhaps the purchase decision will instead respond to practical considerations of functionality, cost, or quality. What type of design element will succeed in forming the type of person-product relationship that promotes brand equity? These questions should be considered at the outset of the design process, and the answers should be incorporated into the design brief.

Examples used in the literature to illustrate the power and breadth of unique design elements include color elements like the robin's-egg blue of Tiffany & Co. and UPS brown. They also include patterns like Levi Strauss' iconic jean pocket stitching. Even scents like the bubblegum scent of Midwest Biologicals' machining oil are cited to illustrate the wide range of unique design elements.[4]

This also applies to the configuration of a product's form, which can be registered trademarks. For example, the Eames Lounge Chair illustrates the long-term value of trade dress protection for furniture product design. Also, "a curvature in the shape of a slight arc" at the top of Zippo's lighter provides a unique feature and a long-lasting commercial advantage. Honeywell's round thermostat, which was awarded a federal trademark registration in 1990 for the design of "a thermostat cover that is circular and rounded in shape," is another example of protectable product design.

Design managers and corporate executives increasingly recognize protected design as an important asset. It is as much an asset as capital equipment. In fact, the value of a firm's physical assets is often exceeded by the value of its inventions, brands, designs, and other IP. One famous example is the hourglass-shaped bottle designed by the Root Glass Company in 1916, which became and remains an immensely valuable design asset of Coca-Cola. Legend has it that the design challenge actually called for a bottle shape that could be recognized even if it were in the dark or broken on the ground.

Working within the parameters of the design challenge and the design brief, the design team should identify preferred modes of design differentiation and then generate design concepts that will promote that differentiation. This provides an opportunity to screen out design concepts that lack significant uniqueness when compared to prior or rival designs. The completion of this early task—the premeditated adoption of unique design elements—should be a required deliverable of the design process and should be specified in the design brief.

Specific guidance about those elements should be provided in the design brief so that they are deliberately introduced into the design. IP counsel can facilitate this process by considering prior and competitive designs to help identify differentiating elements and encouraging designers to incorporate such elements into the design.

Planning for Comprehensive IP Protection

Successful designs will, of course, be emulated or outright copied, and the full commercial value of the original design innovation is thus left unrealized if it can be copied without recourse. IP protections—such as the rights conferred by patents, trademarks, trade dress, and trade secrets—and the strategies used to secure those protections need to be tailored to long-term business objectives. To do so, IP counsel sets strategies to secure comprehensive intellectual property rights, utilizing all available modes of design protection,[5] including protection in countries such as those where a design will be sold or made or licensed.

Virtually all consumer products embody features that perform a function and features that provide a pleasing form. But the legal regimes for protecting design innovations separate form from function. A product can enjoy utility patent or trade secret protection for its functional attributes. Non-functional ornamentation embodied in the same product is instead protected using design patents, and trademark and trade dress protections are available for those non-functional features that can link a product to its source in the minds of consumers.

With respect to a product's shape in particular, trademark and trade dress protections are available for those non-functional features that have acquired secondary meaning in that their appearance has become capable of indicating the source of goods. Unlike utility and design patents, trademarks and trade dress can last as long as they continue to identify a product's source. And with a thoughtful strategy, dual protection of these functional and aesthetic features can help a product achieve iconic status.

Pursuing a Design that Respects Others' IP Rights

With any design effort comes both IP opportunity and IP risk. As noted, there is an opportunity to protect innovations to secure valuable IP rights. Those rights can be used to exclude competitors from adopting the innovation, thereby maintaining a valuable competitive advantage.

At the same time, innovations also bring some risk that commercialization of the new product design may infringe with IP rights of other parties. In other words, it is possible that a design innovation may be within the scope of the protection afforded by another's patent.

Guidance for identifying risks posed by others (e.g., IP rights of competitors and prolific inventors) should be provided in the design brief. IP counsel should be asked to perform a search to identify IP rights of others that may pose risks. The design brief should require the design team to "design around" IP risks and eliminate or reduce them and to communicate them to management.

Building IP Review into the Design Process

Design managers have a unique opportunity to build IP review directly into the design process. This opportunity includes specifying the completion and actions of IP review directly into the design brief. This allows the design team to reap the benefits of an integrated IP strategy while defining a framework for its completion.

Benefits of Integrated IP Strategy

Differentiating design elements should be protected at appropriate times using appropriate IP regimes (e.g., patents, trademarks, copyright). IP risks should be identified, managed, and communicated to management at appropriate times in the design project.

To fully appreciate the role of IP review in design processes, a look at the primary harms of delaying IP review is instructive.

- *Avoid Unanticipated IP Risks* - Delayed IP review deprives the design team of the opportunity to manage the IP risks that may arise from the patent, trade dress, trademark, and copyright rights of others. Failure to identify those risks makes it impossible for the team to avoid them proactively. The late identification of intolerable IP risks can therefore put a halt to the design process, and unanticipated infringement risks can be very difficult to explain to management.

• *Avoid Forfeiting IP Rights* - Delay also deprives the design team of the opportunity to develop a thoughtful strategy for comprehensive IP protection. Without proactive IP review, the team will have little chance to coordinate and execute a plan that utilizes all available modes of IP protection. And because steps must be taken to secure patent protection before certain activities that can bar protection, delay can forfeit valuable IP rights.

• *Avoid Process Inefficiencies* - Addressing IP-related matters only as an afterthought—perhaps just prior to product launch—disrupts the design process. Late IP review often leads to frantic evaluations of the IP rights of others, including hurried patent searches and analyses. All too often, the late discovery of infringement risks results in eleventh-hour design changes and a general atmosphere of uncertainty.

Though most companies now recognize these harms of delay and the benefits of formal IP review, the challenge facing management lies in identifying the best way to integrate IP review into their new product development processes, the actions that need to be taken for proper a IP review, and perhaps most importantly the appropriate timing of these IP-related actions.

Best Practices for Integrated IP Review

Principles of design thinking have helped to integrate business considerations—such as the importance of a strong IP position—into design efforts.[6] The question whether innovation is "designing or thinking" has been aptly answered this way: Designing is thinking.[7] To seize the opportunities afforded by design thinking, it is vital for design managers to integrate IP strategies into their design efforts and to do so by integrating those strategies into their design teams and into the processes that structure their work.

Integration of IP Counsel into the Design Team

Virtually all design processes utilize cross-functional, multidisciplinary design teams formed of individuals from key disciplines that collaborate throughout the design effort. They typically include representatives from the design, engineering, and marketing disciplines but vary based on the nature of the design challenge. An emerging model for integrated IP review formally folds the review of IP risks and opportunities into design processes.[8] But while this model is being embraced with increasing enthusiasm, many companies struggle with the implementation of integrated IP review.

Design managers, working in conjunction with intellectual property counsel, can and should develop strategies to protect the IP rights associated with their design innovations. As a member of the design team, IP counsel ensures that defined steps are taken to identify and then manage IP risks and to strategize and then secure comprehensive IP protection. Like other members of the design team, IP counsel has specific deliverables that must be completed before the project can progress.

Before a design is commercialized, intellectual property counsel also ensures that steps have been taken to protect the design comprehensively. Because designs inevitably evolve between the time they are conceived and the time they are frozen and commercialized, it is important to compare the final design to the design protections that are being pursued to confirm that they are on target. Intellectual property counsel, as part of the design team, can also assess the ability of proposed design elements to be unique and determine the potential strength of that uniqueness.

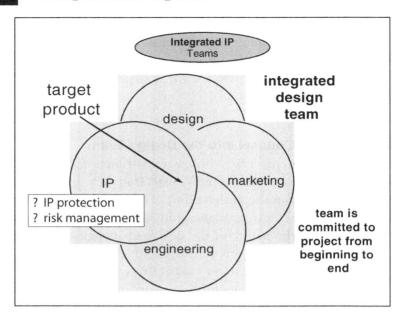

As a design team member, IP counsel makes a number of key contributions. IP counsel will identify and synthesize patents that define the state-of-the-art of the product category, screen out risky product concepts, identify patents that are specifically relevant to the product concept selected by the design team for development, facilitate "design around" efforts in response to identified IP risks, strategize and secure comprehensive IP protection, and memorialize IP analyses.

Integration of IP Review into the Design Process

While identifying the IP-related tasks that need to be completed is important, the question of when those tasks are handled is of equal importance. As noted, delaying these tasks introduces inefficiencies, unanticipated risks, and compromised IP protection. Conversely, they can be handled too early. For example, completing a targeted patent search well before a product design is "frozen" means that later-added features will not be searched and could introduce new risks. It is therefore critical to address IP-related tasks at appropriate junctures in the design process.

The actions required to implement design differentiation strategies should therefore be performed at strategic junctures throughout the design process. Whether a product design effort is considered incremental (such as cost reductions or product improvements), platform (next-generation products), or breakthrough (products new to the company or the world), design processes are generally structured in sequenced stages, the well-known Stage-Gate process being a five-stage, five-gate model. Design differentiation strategies are ideally built into staged processes by incorporating predefined milestones into each stage, thus ensuring that appropriate actions are completed before the design process graduates to the next stage.

As noted in chapter 3, "Essential Elements of the Design Brief," identified phases provide a road map to the design process. These phases may or may not track the stages of a typical Stage-Gate process, but the phases can typically be categorized as those related to concept generation, feasibility, development, and commercialization.

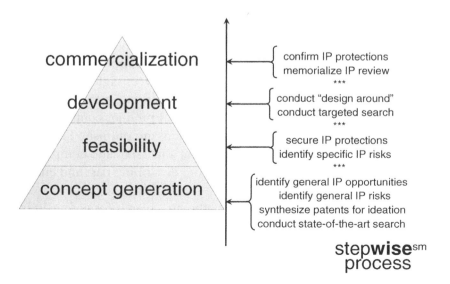

Each design process must be tailored specifically to the needs and culture of the company using it, but design processes generally involve four common sequential phases: concept generation, feasibility study, product development, and commercialization. The design brief should specify the IP activities at each phase.

A Final Word on IP Strategies

When a design enjoys a strong IP position, it can stand out in the marketplace better and benefit from a sustained competitive advantage. When a desired IP position is properly specified in a design brief as a deliverable of the design project, the result is a design that is both protected by IP rights and free of infringing IP rights of others. In that way, the commercial advantage associated with the design innovation can be sustained.

State-of-the-Art Patent Search

A critical contribution of IP counsel is the early identification of patent literature (patents and published patent applications) that is relevant to the product development effort. Over eight million utility patents describe existing technical innovations, more than half a million design patents illustrate ornamental product configurations, and most pending utility patent applications are published eighteen months after they are filed. The result is a massive and comprehensive collection of public patent literature describing past and current innovations.

IP counsel conducts a "state-of-the-art" search for patent literature based on various criteria, including the subject technology for utility patents, ornamentation for design patents, and patent literature of prolific inventors or prospective competitors. The results of the state-of-the-art search are synthesized by IP counsel and presented to the design team well before the product is fully defined. This patent literature will help guide early concept development efforts and identify general patent risks and opportunities.

Screening Out Risky Product Concepts

Once relevant patents are identified, it is critical to screen out risky product concepts that are in danger of infringing patent rights of others. Functional features of certain product concepts may come too close to exclusive rights claimed in a utility patent, and ornamental features of product concepts may resemble a design claimed in a design patent.

Proactive identification of patent infringement risks and the early elimination of risky product concepts streamline the design process. This early filtration of product concepts allows the team to turn away from concepts that should not be pursued and allows the team to focus its attention on surviving product concepts.

Targeted Patent Search

In contrast to (and perhaps supplementing) the state-of-the-art search performed earlier in the process, a "targeted" search of the patent literature is conducted by IP counsel to identify patents specifically relevant to the product concept ultimately selected by the design team for development. Once the features of a selected product concept are nearly "frozen," those features can be searched to identify any specific infringement risks that they may bring. This search targets unexpired patents and published patent applications that may claim exclusive rights to features of the product under consideration.

"Designing Around"

Armed with the knowledge gained by the searches, IP counsel leads a "design around" effort for those aspects of a product concept most at risk of infringing the patent rights of others. To do so, IP counsel evaluates the scope of protection provided by a relevant patent and helps the design team to navigate around that scope.

The "design around" process therefore identifies design modifications that reduce or eliminate infringement risks. Though mostly defensive in nature at its outset, this process very often leads to new innovations.

Securing Comprehensive IP Rights

Because the commercial success of many products depends not only on how they function but also on their aesthetic appeal, IP counsel sets strategies to secure comprehensive IP rights, utilizing all available modes of IP protection.

IP counsel ensures that IP protections are in place prior to product launch, including foreign patent protection where a product will be sold overseas or if value can be derived from licensing the product innovation to foreign companies. IP counsel will also ensure that steps have been taken to establish other IP rights, including trademark, trade secret, and copyright protections, as appropriate. And at product launch, IP counsel initiates procedures for monitoring the activities of competitors and policing the IP rights generated by the design team.

Memorializing IP Assessments

It is prudent for IP counsel to memorialize the reasons why the product does not infringe any identified patents of particular relevance. This may require the preparation of a formal written opinion with a detailed legal analysis of the patent and its history at the Patent Office.

Documentation of a good-faith belief that the product does not infringe the IP rights of others will help shield the company from accusations of bad faith and willful infringement. Such a shield is especially valuable in the event that the product is actually found to infringe patent rights in litigation and damages are assessed for that infringement.

Concept Generation

In this early phase, product concepts are generated and selected based on input from the design team. IP input in this phase facilitates concept review and fosters ideation.

The "state-of-the-art" search, conducted early in this phase by IP counsel, catalyzes ideation in the design team by exposing it to prior efforts of others. This is in fact a fundamental objective of our patent system, which encourages inventors to promptly and thoroughly reveal their innovations in order to make innovations available for improvement by others. While the state-of-the-art search educates the design team about the prior efforts of others, a company's own patent portfolio can provide an additional starting point when looking into new products or expanding into new business opportunities. IP counsel is instrumental in "mining" such a portfolio for patents of interest to the team.

State-of-the-art patent searches also reveal general areas of IP-related risk early in the concept phase, including prospective infringement risks, future competitors, and potentially blocking patents owned by others. IP counsel's early identification of general risk areas in the concept phase helps the design team to navigate IP minefields.

Early patent searches can also reveal fruitful IP-related opportunities. Partners or merger targets may be identified, and the patent literature will help the design team to develop proactive strategies for acquiring IP protection from others (by license or assignment), to explore areas for prospective patent protection, and to identify technologies that are already available for all to use.

Feasibility Study

While marketing professionals ask whether it is feasible to promote selected product concepts in the feasibility phase of the design process, engineers and designers consider whether it is feasible to develop the concepts within cost, performance, and aesthetic constraints. And IP counsel answers the important question whether the product concepts generated earlier in the concept phase are legally feasible. This is accomplished by identifying patent risks that are specific to the concepts under consideration and by beginning to formulate strategies for IP protection.

If specific risks are identified, IP counsel helps the design team to screen out any risky concepts or "design around" an identified infringement risk. These efforts are best made in this early feasibility phase to avoid late-stage product revisions.

IP counsel also leads the team's efforts to protect selected product concepts. By taking proactive steps to file patent applications in the feasibility stage, patent protection is sought before concepts are shown to prospective suppliers and customers. Predating such disclosures preserves foreign and domestic patent rights. If a design concept must be disclosed (for Voice of the Customer [VoC] review or to communicate with vendors for example), IP counsel prepares non-disclosure agreements for use by the design team.

Product Development

IP counsel helped the design team to eliminate risky product concepts in the feasibility phase, and a product concept acceptable to all members of the design team has now been selected for development. Because the product is now defined, a targeted search is conducted to identify any patent claims of specific relevance to the features of the proposed product.

If patents are identified that pose a risk of infringement, IP counsel continues the "design around" function by identifying design modifications that place the ultimate product outside the scope of the patent rights of others. Again, this proactive identification and management of infringement risks reduces late-stage surprises.

Commercialization

In the commercialization phase, the now-completed product design is readied for launch. IP counsel memorializes the assessments conducted in earlier phases and ensures that IP protection has been pursued.

Before product launch (or even before any capital expenditures are made to ready the product for launch), structured design processes require formal legal clearance and confirmation that any risks associated with the launch of the product are tolerable. This often requires the preparation and completion of one or more formal written opinions.

Before launch, IP counsel also ensures that IP protections have been initiated and are adequate to protect the product comprehensively. And at product launch, IP counsel will initiate procedures for monitoring the activities of competitors for possible infringement of those IP protections.

Chapter 12

An Example of a Design Brief

At every presentation of my DMI seminar on design briefs, invariably one or more people ask if I can show them a "perfect" design brief. The simple answer is, no, I cannot. There are several reasons for this. First of all, there is no such thing as a single example of a "perfect design brief." A design brief becomes *perfect* only when you have constructed it very carefully with your co-owner/partner and it has performed well for you for a *specific* project. *Then*, you might call it perfect.

The next most important reason I can't show a perfect, real example is that no company in its right mind would let me publish such a brief in a book or distribute copies at a seminar. As you now know, a really good design brief contains a great deal of proprietary information about a company's business strategy, results of research data, and future plans. This is not the kind of information companies are willing to share. Design briefs are highly confidential documents. Although I have personally seen a great many good design briefs, and I certainly have been part of the development of hundreds of them, the companies I have worked with always have me sign confidentiality agreements that prohibit sharing their information outside of that company.

The best I can do is to completely fabricate a fictitious brief for an imaginary company. What follows is just such an imaginary brief. I have used the information for the background and objectives section from a real company that I quoted in chapter 3 as a starting point. It is a fairly typical design problem for some companies, and the source (the name of the company) is completely transparent. From there, I have fabricated everything else. My only purpose is to demonstrate about how long a brief might be if you only included the basics I covered in chapter 3. I have added some annotations for each section as a type of review of the critical elements. It would also be best to assume that this would be the first draft presented to the design brief project team for discussion and approval. Such a team might want to add some material, revise the wording, or delete some material, as I described earlier. Once again, think of this only as an example of a *starting point* for a brief.

I have also chosen to use the narrative format, since that is the one I personally favor. Remember, you can develop any format you like, as long as it is clear and works well for you and your company.

Please do not assume that this example is in any way reflective of any particular company or industry category. It is just an example.

ACME COMPANY

Design Brief
Total Redesign of Company Portfolio

Project Overview and Background

The current company portfolio reflects a series of different visual treatments that were created at various points in time to fulfill various business objectives and strategies. As a result, the portfolio lacks visual cohesiveness and clarity. This exacerbates target audience confusion within the complicated and already cluttered global marketplace for these products. In order to achieve clarity and cohesiveness, and to shorten the sales cycle, increase competitive advantage, improve market share, and thus enhance the bottom line, the entire portfolio must be redesigned at one time, utilizing an umbrella strategy. Design principles and strategy for future new products must also be established within this umbrella strategy.

The ultimate design solution will consistently incorporate company branding elements, achieve a cohesive visual appearance across the line, and clearly distinguish the different products within this umbrella strategy.

In order to most efficiently execute this project, the redesign will be conducted in eight phases:

- Phase 1—Complete visual audit of existing company portfolio as well as a visual audit of the top three competitors' portfolios.
- Phase 2—Develop a maximum of six creative design concepts that meet project business objectives.
- Phase 3—Test all concepts with target audiences.
- Phase 4—Select three concepts and further refine each. Retest all three with target audience.
- Phase 5—Select one concept, fully develop it, and perform final testing.
- Phase 6—Develop approval presentation.
- Phase 7—Implement approved design solution.
- Phase 8—Develop measurement metrics.

The project is scheduled to be completed by (date). The budget for this project has been set at (amount).

Project owners shall be (name), vice president of marketing, and (name), strategic design director.

Design brief project team members will include: (list of names/titles of each team member)

Note: The only change I have made to the presentation of this portion of the example design brief in chapter 3 is to add the last phases, as I discussed earlier. As mentioned before, this section also serves as the executive summary of the project.

Category Review

The ABC category is a $60 billion industry worldwide. Although there are more than 125 brands competing in this category, only four brands are considered market leaders. These four brands collectively account for 65 percent of the total market.

Brand X is the current market leader, with a 25.5 percent share of the market. Brand X was the third company to enter this category when the category was developed forty-seven years ago. Within seven years, Brand X had acquired the first two competitors to enter the market, making Brand X the dominant brand worldwide. Within five years of Brand X's initial acquisitions, more than thirty other companies entered the rapidly growing category. Demand for these new products by consumers more than doubled each year for the first decade. Brand X had achieved dominance primarily because it was one of the original brands in the category; it had the widest distribution system, which ensured their products were available virtually everywhere; and it had very high brand recognition and recall by the target audience.

Brand Y is the second largest competitor, with a 15.5 percent total share of the current market. Brand Y has achieved its current position primarily through very aggressive marketing and promotion techniques. Brand Y utilizes extensive couponing and discounting programs worldwide, making their offerings appear somewhat less expensive than the others.

Brand Z and our company, ACME, are tied for third place, with a market share of 12 percent each. Brand Z is somewhat older than the number two brand, Y. Brand Z has been in the market for twenty-eight years, and Brand Y has been in the market for twenty years. Brand Z has wide distribution, primarily through mass market discount chains worldwide. Brand Z's product line is considered less expensive than the other leading brands. Brand Z competes primarily on price considerations.

ACME Company is sixteen years old. Our company has achieved its number three position largely through aggressive marketing and advertising focusing on superior quality and craftsmanship. ACME has not traditionally offered deep discounting and does not use coupons in the marketplace. ACME products are priced at parity with Brands X and Y.

The balance of the competitors in the marketplace have generally existed less than ten years as a brand, and most of them tend to be more regional than national or global.

Although demand for these products grew rapidly for nearly twenty years, the market is now declining slightly. This is primarily due to a weak economy in most parts of the world and shifting consumer needs.

Industry business analysts predict that many competitors will gradually drop out of the market over the next five years. Some brands will be acquired by the top three brands, and others will simply cease doing business. Analysts predict that no more than twelve brands will ultimately survive in the marketplace.

It is incumbent on the top four brands, including ACME Company, to ensure their continued presence in the marketplace by strengthening their positions through product improvements and more compelling "reasons to purchase."

Notes: More than likely, the content of this section has come from a market research group or other marketing function within the company. So just why is this category review description helpful to designers? Primarily because it is a brief summary of what has happened as well as what is happening right now in the category. One of the important points that a designer or design team could take away from this particular example is that the market is quite large—$60 billion. This is particularly significant because it means the category has major visibility in the consumer market place. Obviously people are looking for these products worldwide.

A designer should also recognize that with 125 brands competing, there must be a great deal of visual clutter in this space, and that means the design must be visually prominent, distinctive, and "different" from all of these competitors. However, we learn that there are only four major brands. And we learn that ACME is tied for number three in total market share. This signals that ACME primarily needs to study these four brands very carefully in their visual audit.

It should also be significant to designers that the category is nearly a half-century old. The category leader is forty-seven years old. This means that it has considerable brand equity in its visual appearance and might encounter difficulties if it tried to come up with a "whole new look." ACME also has this problem. ACME is a quarter of a century old, and also enjoys strong visual equity in its brand. Translation: ACME needs to proceed with caution if it tries to stray too far from its established brand identification.

Another critical area to designers in this category review is that the vast majority of competitors are relatively new, and therefore not as well known as the leaders. They would have considerably more freedom than the current category leaders in presenting themselves as highly contemporary, forward-thinking, leading-edge, and even "experimental."

We also learn that the number one brand in the category has traditionally been very aggressive in the marketplace. It has bought out the early market leaders to eliminate that competition. It is constantly promoting with discount offers. This means it is trying to maintain its position by a reduced price strategy. It is also everywhere! Its superior distribution system ensures that no matter what store a consumer goes into, that brand is always available. Therefore, it is easy to find and easy to purchase. ACME has followed a business strategy of not discounting in favor of a message that it is the highest-quality producer and therefore worth the premium price of the product. As ACME designers begin to develop concepts for redesigning the whole portfolio, this fact will be critical. Their new designs will have to carry through this theme of "superior quality."

Finally, the category has flattened out. It is more than likely that there will not be many new brands entering the market; in fact, many current brands may cease to exist in a few years. ACME Company will most likely survive, so it needs to be sure to consider some classical, more timeless design concepts. While newer companies can explore highly contemporary design treatments, ACME will need to ensure its new design concepts are not trendy or fads of the moment. In 2015, ACME cannot afford to have people saying that ACME looks like a 2003 brand, or that ACME is old-fashioned. On the other hand, ACME does want to make its visual image more contemporary, while still communicating that it is are well established and has been around for a very long time.

All of these points, and possibly others, will need to be discussed by the design team prior to exploring concept development. The category is complex. ACME will need to look fresh and up-to-date, but not trendy. The message of superior quality will have to come through loud and clear in all treatments. ACME will need to leverage its heritage, but at the same time update its image. Obviously, all of this creates a major design challenge. The category review is well worth the time it will take to discuss in depth!

Most likely, your company's market research group or marketing group will provide most of this category review for you. It is then up to the design brief project team, as well as the design team, to analyze the category review for clues that will help them develop initial concepts.

Target Audience Review

ACME Company's product line is considered a basic necessity for the care and maintenance of living quarters. Nearly every apartment, private home, hotel, inn, and so forth, will have one or more of these devices. For this reason, the target audience does not include young children or individuals living in someone else's home. Generally, the youngest male or female who would purchase or use one of these products is college-age (eighteen years plus) and occupying his or her first living space away from home. These younger individuals tend to purchase our lower-priced models, which are very basic devices. As the target audience, consisting of both males and females, sets up more permanent housekeeping, this audience tends to look for either our mid-priced models, or possibly our most expensive models. The average age of consumers in this latter category is twenty-four to thirty years old. As our target audience matures, it will tend to give more consideration to our more expensive models, which have a variety of options available. The average age of individuals who consider this type of upgrade is forty to sixty years.

While the primary purchase decision maker was female twenty or more years ago, today both sexes can be considered primary decision makers.

The degree of sophistication and education of those who purchase our product is important. Our superior models, with a wide array of options, tend to be purchased by individuals with college degrees beyond the bachelor's level. The basic models, purchased by all age groups, are more likely to be purchased by individuals who want simplicity of operation, basic performance, and low cost.

Specialized versions of our product line, especially the very small handheld units, have more appeal to individuals who live in motor homes, or for use on boats. These handheld models are also popular with college students who live in dormitory rooms or studio-sized apartments.

Another category of the target audience that must be considered is professionals who are hired to maintain larger living spaces or office buildings. This category prefers the larger, more "industrial strength" models, regardless of initial cost.

Our product line is considered a consumer durable product; therefore, individuals only purchase an average of four units in their lifetime. The market trend is for people to initially purchase a basic, low-cost model, and then upgrade two or three times to the more advanced models. Income levels of the target audience tend to increase in ten-year intervals, beginning at the lower end of age twenty to thirty, advancing each subsequent decade, and leveling off at approximately age sixty. Elderly people (ages seventy plus) often return to the basic models because of their ease of use and low cost.

For all segments of the target audience, consumers are most interested in: ease of use, durability, overall performance, cost, warranty, readily available repair service, and functionality.

The younger consumers (eighteen to thirty) are most interested in sporting events, social events with peers, watching videos, popular music, and domestic travel. Our target audience in the age group between thirty and fifty report that its primary interests include: foreign travel, outdoor events including skiing, aquatic sports, boating, reading, attending cultural events such as the theater, and home improvement projects. Consumers over the age of fifty tend to spend more time at home (or in a vacation home), watching television, reading, and participating in community activities.

Note: This section also provides a great deal of useful information for the design team. ACME Company has several tiers of its basic product, from low-end models to "industrial strength" and luxury models. The typical ages, income, interests, and level of education and sophistication are described for each tier of the product line. It is always important to remember that this kind of audience description is always based on averages from market research. It can never be absolute. It is meant more as a guideline. For example, there could very well be a young consumer who wants, and can afford, the most luxurious model of the product, even for his dorm room at college.

However, for a project such as this one, it is necessary for the designers to discuss each of the types of audience described as typical for a particular product. For example, how would—or should—package design differ for each group in the target audience? What are the implications from the comment that both males and females buy the product? Does this mean graphic concepts should be gender neutral? Why or why not?

Another interesting point for discussion that could be extracted from this target audience review is that the basic models appeal primarily to very young consumers who are entering the market for the first time, as well as to the very elderly consumer who is no stranger to the market and has used the product for years. What does this mean to a design team? Should the various design elements of the product (the product itself, the packaging, the sales collateral material, etc.) be geared more toward one age group than the other? How can the design become appealing to both groups? How big an issue is this anyway? What are we going to do about it? How should we approach this issue?

These design concept discussions have to come from the material supplied largely by marketing people who did not have design specifically in mind when they did their research. This becomes another added value of a strategic design function—to take largely marketing-driven research and extract design strategy from what is available. As I mentioned in chapter 3, this is why a short phrase in response to target audience description, such as "women twenty to fifty," isn't useful to a design team. There just isn't any jumping-off place for meaningful, strategic design discussion.

Company Portfolio

The entire ACME Company portfolio consists of 100 discrete stock-keeping units (SKUs). This project will not involve the redesign of any product. Rather, the redesign project will focus only on packaging, collateral sales literature, retail in-store display items, catalogs, and owners' manuals. The 100 SKUs include:

- **Basic Line:** one full-size unit, one handheld unit, one commercial full-size unit, and one commercial handheld unit, for a total of four discrete products. These are well-engineered basic units with no frills, accessories, or other options.

  They are the lowest-cost units, with a suggested retail price of $40 for the basic full-size unit, $30 for the basic handheld unit, $65 for the heavy-duty full-size basic commercial unit, and $55 for the commercial handheld unit.

- **Mid-price Line:** one full-size unit, one handheld unit, one commercial full-size unit, and one commercial handheld unit, for a total of four discrete products. In addition, each of these four mid-price units are available with up to five optional attachments, each sold and priced separately. Including the optional attachments, the mid-price line includes a total of twenty-four SKUs. The entire mid-price line has slightly better engineering of components. The optional attachments are not compatible with any product in the basic line.

  The mid-price line suggested retail price is $125 for the full-size unit, and $175 for the commercial full-size unit. Handheld versions are priced at $100 and $140 for the commercial unit. The five optional accessories for each of these products are priced from $30 to $80 each, depending upon the functionality of the accessory.

- **Luxury Line:** one full-size unit, one handheld unit, one commercial full-size unit, and one commercial handheld unit, for a total of four discrete products in the luxury line. In addition, each of the standard items in the line are available with up to five optional attachments, each priced separately. The luxury line also includes three color options: white, gray, and blue. The color options are available for both the main unit as well as the optional accessories. The luxury line consists of seventy-two SKUs, including accessory options and color options.

The luxury line suggested retail price is $430 for the main unit and $550 for the commercial version. The handheld units retail for $375 and $500 for the commercial version. Accessories range in price from $80 to $250, depending on the accessory. There is no additional charge for choice of color. The luxury line features state-of-the-art engineering, highest-quality components, a lifetime warranty for parts and labor for any component that fails due to manufacturing defects, and a standard leather storage bag for both the main product as well as the accessories.

ACME Company utilizes a monolithic brand strategy with all products employing the ACME brand. ACME is not involved with any other type of product. ACME Company is publicly held and governed by a board of directors elected by shareholders. Stock prices have risen to a high of $93 over the past year. Current stock price for the last quarter is $57.

ACME's primary competitors offer essentially the same range of products and accessories. Brand X, the market leader, does offer limited accessories for its basic line of products. Brand X also heavily promotes its commercial line of products to noncommercial consumers. Brand Y does not offer accessories for its basic line of products; Brand Y often offers one or more free accessories for its mid-price and luxury lines during special product promotion periods. Brand Z occasionally offers deep discounts for short periods, such as just prior to the Christmas holidays. Brand Z never offers free accessories and does not even offer accessories for its basic line of products.

ACME is currently tied for the number three position in the marketplace with Brand Z. Each company has a 12 percent share of the market. (Please refer to the category review section for more details on the leading four competitors.)

ACME Company's business strategy is to compete in the market by offering the highest degree of quality, value, and craftsmanship.

The company does not compete on price considerations. The business strategy is based on the assumption that consumers will pay a higher price for superior quality. ACME Company is sixteen years old. The first decade was a period of growth beginning with the basic unit and expanding through three tiers to the luxury unit. Accessories and color choices were introduced seven years ago.

The period of rapid expansion of product offerings has ended for the immediate future. Corporate management has made a decision to end expansion of the product line and to focus on improving quality, craftsmanship, and reliability of ACME's products. This decision is in keeping with the overall business philosophy of competing in the marketplace solely on the basis of superior quality and value to the consumer.

ACME's products are sold worldwide. Minor variations to the design of the products themselves, as well as to the design the sales collateral materials, in-store display items, catalogs, and owners' manuals, have been made to satisfy various geographical requirements.

Market research has demonstrated that the ACME product line is not always perceived clearly by the consumer. During the product line's period of rapid expansion, particularly with the introduction of the luxury line, color choices, and accessories—the visual manifestation of the master brand—ACME was diluted and fragmented. Some consumers have complained that as they wish to add optional accessories, the packaging confuses them. They are not always sure that a particular accessory is compatible with their standard unit and its particular model year. ACME's three prime competitors make a claim that their accessories are compatible with—and superior to—ACME's accessories. These competitors often use the ACME name on their accessory packaging with a disclaimer, "Compatible with all ACME brand products." These competitors' accessories are priced much lower than ACME's accessories. In an attempt to alleviate this confusion, senior management at ACME Company has directed that the entire portfolio of product literature, packaging, in-store display units, and catalogs be redesigned to allow consumers to quickly and readily identify a "genuine ACME Company product." The ultimate goal is to ensure that the ACME brand is instantly identifiable by consumers, and that the business philosophy of ensuring the highest quality and value is clear to the various target audiences worldwide.

Notes: The company portfolio section is most valuable because it clearly defines the breadth of the project. In this example, the design team is able to succinctly convey what artifacts are to be redesigned, a description of each product, competitive product line components, and marketing and promotion techniques utilized by ACME and its competitors. This section also further explains ACME's management philosophy and business strategy.

A design team that is meeting to discuss this brief would undoubtedly want to make a large chart. Across the top, horizontally, I would suggest listing the components of the redesign: sales literature, in-store display, catalogs, packaging, and owners' manuals. Down the vertical axis, I would list each of the 100 SKUs described. The task would then be to discuss each item on the chart. If the first SKU listed in the vertical column was the full-size basic unit, and the first column in the horizontal unit was headlined "Sales Literature," the team would now have an area of focus for discussion. I would list the sales literature currently available for the full-size basic unit from ACME Company, then list the sales literature available from the other three competitors for their basic units. I would proceed in the same way for each SKU and each category in the redesign project. You can see this will be time-consuming—but at the same time, critical!

The result will be a giant matrix that will clearly show the overall scope of the work, the materials you will need to assemble for a visual audit, and the company's areas of strength and vulnerability. You will really need to do some exercise like this one prior to considering your overall design strategy. The project could be thought of as a giant jigsaw puzzle. You will need to assemble all of the pieces, then attempt to solve the puzzle in a coherent and logical manner.

This type of process will also be critical to creating detail for the description, time line, and budget for each phase.

If this particular project had been described only as a redesign of one tier, say, the luxury tier of products, you would probably want to do this complete exercise anyway. It does not make sense to redesign just one product, or one group of products, without understanding how these products fit with the rest of the company portfolio.

Now for some good news! Why not start right now to develop your own design group company portfolio chart? Why wait for a project to come along? I am aware of design groups in several companies that have done this as a matter of routine. These design groups tell me that just designing this company portfolio chart, and keeping it updated as new products are introduced and others are eliminated, has made an enormous difference in all of their design work.

One Fortune 50 company I have worked with constructed a special room for this kind of activity. Whole walls were covered with examples or photographs of each of their products, and the visual support materials for each product. Prime competitive material was integrated with their own materials. This had been the design group's idea and was primarily created as a design resource. However, as word about this room spread, people from just about every function in the company came to visit the display. Both marketing and sales said that it was the most useful company presentation they had ever seen. The CEO was ecstatic. Not a bad way to get positive recognition for design within the company, and save yourself an awful lot of time developing design brief content!

Business Objectives and Design Strategy

Business Objectives	Design Strategy
Restore visual cohesiveness and clarity to company portfolio of products in order to strengthen brand recognition among consumers.	Develop a unique grid system that will be used consistently with every application across all three tiers. Develop a standard typographic system that will be used consistently with every application. Develop a color palette that will be used consistently for all products. Explore concepts that will utilize specific color coding for each tier of products.

	Explore concepts that will utilize various forms of imagery to define products (e.g. photography, illustration, and image concepts that include people using the product, as well as concepts that feature the product only).
Ensure that ACME Company's products are clearly differentiated, visually, from all competitors.	Audit all major competitors for use of specific visual elements and style. Develop design concepts that are uniquely different from all competitors' while still communicating "superior quality."
Improve market share and the bottom line.	Develop design concepts that have the key objectives of making all products instantly recognizable as ACME brand products, make each tier attractive to the specific target audience for the particular tier, and powerfully reinforce the primary messages of superior quality and value.
Enhance equity in the ACME brand by maintaining corporate brand identity standards.	Develop design concepts that display the corporate logo prominently and consistently across the entire product line. Build on brand heritage by not altering the brand logo in any way, but also allowing the brand to appear more contemporary by utilizing the brand logo in more contemporary physical environments.
Establish design guidelines for the possibility of future new products being added to the company portfolio when the market recovers.	Develop design concepts that are representative of current fads or trends in design. Pursue design concepts that are more "classical" in approach without appearing "old-fashioned" or dated.

(Continued)

	Determine what types of new products might be anticipated, and what the target audience for these new products might be. Develop a design house style guide that could endure for at least ten years.
Clearly distinguish each value tier: • basic • basic commercial/ low end • mid-price • luxury models	Develop concepts that maintain a cohesive visual appearance of the brand across the entire company portfolio but still allowing for use of various individual graphic devices for each value tier.

Note: Please note that the design strategies listed do not specifically describe any particular design element or concept. Rather, this section simply lists those business objectives that the company feels are critical to the outcomes of this project and ensures that there is an agreed to design strategy for each one. As mentioned in chapter 3, these design strategies may be changed as work begins on concept development. That's okay. This is simply a jumping-off point. The business objectives may also change. Usually, this takes the form of adding business objectives, not deleting them. If a business objective is added, it will more than likely alter some of the initial design strategies.

However, the goal is to minimize the number of changes, or—hopefully—to eliminate them altogether. The design strategies should be discussed with the design team prior to including them in the first draft of the design brief. As a possible exercise in your own design group, try taking the business objectives outlined in this list and seeing what design strategies your own group might come up with. More than likely, they will be different from the ones used in this example!

Project Scope, Time Line, and Budget

Note: In the following example, the design group is presumed to be an in-house corporate design group that is centrally funded by the corporation. All design staff are salaried employees; therefore, no budget has been assigned to this project for design staff labor (time). Salaried employees are generally not eligible for overtime pay. In most instances, the centrally funded group's employee salary and benefit overhead is not charged back to specific design projects. If this project were to be executed by an external design firm, or an in-house group that operates on a charge-back system for staff time, employee overhead would have to be calculated into the project cost. Obviously, this would make the budget for the specific project a great deal higher.

- Phase 1—*Comprehensive visual audit of existing company portfolio, as well as a visual audit of the top three competitors' portfolios.* This phase will include:
  - Assembling one copy of each ACME Company catalog, unit of sales collateral literature, current in-store display unit, package, owner's manual, and product.
  - Assembling one copy of each of the above for Brands X, Y, and Z. (Note: The corporate strategic design group already has all of this material from ACME Company and the competitors as it is gathered on a routine basis. Therefore, very little time will be required to assemble this material.)
  - Design team to conduct a visual audit of all material listed. Time frame for this activity will be five full business days (forty hours). The strategic design manager and the four designers (names should be listed) will conduct this initial audit. Because of our funding structure, and because all materials are currently available, there is no direct cost to the project for this activity.
  - The strategic design group shall prepare a written report of the findings from this audit. In particular, this report shall contain detailed information about how the audit results relate to the stated business objectives of this project, as well as the apparent strengths and weaknesses of the design elements utilized by Brands X, Y, and Z.

    The design audit results document shall be prepared by the strategic design manager, (<u>name</u>), and the lead designer of the design project team, (<u>name</u>). This audit report will require three business days to prepare. There is no cost to the project for development of this report, as the design function is centrally funded.

- Both hard copies and electronic copies of this report shall be distributed to the entire design team, the design brief project team, all previously identified project stakeholders, and all approvers who will be listed for each phase of the project. The completed visual audit report shall also become a part of the appendix of this design brief.

    Materials used for the visual audit shall be maintained by the strategic design group and made available to anyone within the company who wishes to review the material on his own. The cost of duplication, distribution (postage and handling by a document distribution company contracted by ACME Company), and storage of the materials will be $600. The report distribution company will require two business days for copying and distribution.

- The visual audit report will be reviewed by (<u>name</u>), co-owner/partner of the project (previously identified as the vice president of marketing), the vice president of sales, the international marketing director, and the entire design brief project team. A meeting of this entire team will be scheduled to review their comments and concerns six business days after the distribution of the report. At the conclusion of this meeting, the design brief project team will approve the visual audit document.

- The total time frame for this phase shall be seventeen business days (including the six business days for individual review by key stakeholders). The total cost for this phase will be $600.

- Phase 2—Develop a maximum of six creative design concepts that meet business objectives. Working as a team, four designers from the strategic design group, under the overall direction of the strategic design manager, will develop a maximum of six creative concepts for presentation to the design brief project team for approval. More than six creative design concepts will be explored, but only six will be selected for presentation. The selected concepts will all address the business objectives, the design strategy, and the results of the visual audit.

The development and refinement of six design concepts for presentation will require six weeks of time by the design team. Expenses for external vendors of supplies and materials for this concept development project will not exceed $50,000. Typical examples of these external expenses include, photography, model-making (for in-store display units), supplies for graphic design work, and some travel, lodging, and per diem out-of-pocket expense reimbursements for the design staff, who may have to engage in some limited travel.

Key stakeholders who will be routinely consulted during this concept development process include representatives from sales, marketing, law, the various global geographies, market research, external vendors for printing, display fabrication, package engineering, and manufacturing.

At the conclusion of this initial concept development phase, the design team shall present the six concepts to the entire design brief project team for discussion and approval. Once the design brief project team has granted approval, we will proceed to the next phase.

Phase 2 will require six weeks of concept development time and one week for design brief project team discussion and approval. The total time for phase two is seven weeks. The total budget for phase two is $50,000.

- Phase 3—*Test all concepts with target audiences.* PDF files of the six approved design concepts will be sent to sales and marketing executives in all regions and geographies. When practical, models of display units will also be sent to these representatives. Each representative will be asked to show all six concepts to at least five people from the target audience for each tier. No information will be given to the members of the target audience. They will only be asked, "Could you please give me your immediate reaction to each of these design treatments?"

Verbal responses are all that is required. These should be recorded on audiotape for each interview. Target audience interviews should take no more than fifteen to twenty minutes for each person interviewed. The objective is to obtain top-of-mind immediate responses to each design concept from the target audience. Written and audiotape recorded responses should be sent to the strategic design director at (<u>name and address</u>). Company representatives shall have three weeks to complete these interviews. Transcripts of these test results will be added to the appendix of this design brief.

The total time allotted to phase 3 is four weeks: one week for distribution of materials and three weeks for interviews. The budget for phase 3, including duplication and distribution of the materials, is $5,000.

- Phase 4—*Select three concepts and further refine each.* Retest all three with target audience. Based on worldwide target audience testing of the initial six design concepts, the design brief project team, in collaboration with the design team, will select three design concepts for further refinement. The design team will require three weeks for this refinement process. The cost of this further refinement process will be $35,000. This budget will cover the same categories of items as described in phase 2.

Upon refining three of the original design concepts, all three will be tested in an identical manner as described in phase 3. Once again, the testing process will require four weeks and an expenditure of $5,000 of the total budget. These test result transcripts will also be added to the appendix of this design brief.

The total time for phase 4 will be seven weeks, and the total budget for phase 4 will be $40,000.

- Phase 5 —*Select one concept, fully develop it, and perform final testing.* The results of the phase 4 design concept testing will be analyzed and discussed by the design brief project team and the design team. One concept will be approved for final development and ultimate presentation to senior management for approval. The four members of the design team shall collaborate producing comprehensives and models for this design solution.

Key stakeholders who will be involved in this phase 5 work other than the design brief team include:

- The law department for final legal review
- A representative from marketing from each major geography worldwide
- A representative from procurement
- All external vendors who will manufacture or produce the components of the project
- A representative from sales for all major geographies
- A representative from the corporate distribution function
- A representative from the finance function, who will produce a final accounting analysis for the project

In addition to fully developing the selected design concept by the design team, each key stakeholder will be accountable for producing a written plan for implementation of the project from his or her functional perspective:

- Sales and marketing will develop internal and external communication plans
- Procurement will begin the process of preparing vendor bids and awarding contracts
- The law department will prepare a written opinion concerning any legal issues
- Distribution will prepare a definitive plan for replacing existing materials in the distribution system with the new materials once they are available
- Finance will prepare a full financial report for the project, to be available at the time of presentation to senior management for final approval.
- Phase 5 will require eight weeks to complete. The final design development process has been budgeted at $100,000. At the conclusion of the final development of a design solution, an external testing agency will be engaged to professionally test the solution with the target audience worldwide. The testing agency will be given four weeks for testing and preparing a report on the test results. The budget for external testing has been set at $100,000.

The total time frame for phase 5 is twelve weeks. The total budget, including the cost of testing, has been set at $200,000. The external agency test result summaries will be added to the appendix of this design brief.

At the conclusion of phase 5, the design team, the external testing agency, and the entire design brief project team shall meet to formally approve the design solution. This meeting will be scheduled as a full-day meeting. One week prior to this meeting, all members of the design brief project team shall be sent PDF files of the design solution, the test results, and all formal written plans produced by additional key stakeholders. This will allow the design brief project team to attend the final approval meeting with substantive knowledge of the entire plan, as well as the business rationale for the approval of the final design solution that the team previously selected.

- Phase 6—*Develop approval presentation.* The co-owners of the project will be accountable for preparing a senior management approval presentation and for making this presentation to (<u>name</u>) on (<u>date and time</u>). The design team will prepare all visual artifacts for this approval presentation. The final approver will be sent all materials, including the design brief and all reports from key stakeholders, one week prior to the final approval presentation.

  The co-owners of the project will require two weeks for preparation of this approval presentation. The budget for the development and production of the approval presentation is $8,000.

- Phase 7—*Implement approved design solution.* In order to implement the approved new design concept for the entire project line in a short period of time, a subcommittee of the design brief project team shall be formed to develop an implementation plan.

  This plan shall include specific instructions for rapid liquidation of current supplies of printed collateral sales literature, catalogs, owners' manuals, and packaging. Additionally, this plan will include the consumer communications plan and a new sales and marketing plan for the rollout, in addition to describing any variations required by different geographies. The implementation plan will become an integral part of the senior management's final approval presentation. This detailed implementation plan will be developed during the same time period as the final approval presentation as described in phase 6 (total time two weeks). Since each of the corporate functions will develop its portion of the implementation plan individually, no budget has been assigned to this activity.

The goal is to achieve full worldwide implementation of the new company portfolio design within one business quarter (three months). Manufacturing and distribution of the new materials, as well as disposal of the current manifestations of all artifacts, is estimated to cost $1,000,000.

- Phase 8—Develop measurement metrics. Based on the stated and approved business objectives for this project, measurement metrics have been developed by the design brief project team. (Name of company) has been contracted to conduct monthly surveys by telephone of typical customers worldwide. Twelve hundred customers and prospective customers will be contacted each month. These surveys will continue for a period of two years. Results of each monthly survey will be made available to the design brief project team and ACME senior management on a monthly basis.

These surveys will measure reaction to a standard group of questions designed to determine: unaided awareness of the ACME brand, unaided awareness of Brands X, Y, and Z; recall and understanding of key messages and reasons to buy, as put forth by the aforementioned competitors as well as by ACME Company; and likelihood of a preference for each of these brands. The complete questionnaire and specific details concerning this testing are included in the appendix of this design brief. Key findings will address the following questions:

- Is the ACME brand clear to members of the target audience for each product line tier?

- What percentage of the target audience recognizes and is aware of the ACME brand?
- How do consumers differentiate the offerings of the top four brands in the market?
- Do consumers easily recognize the different value tiers through visual means?
- How long has each respondent been aware of the ACME brand?
- Has the respondent's opinion of the ACME brand changed in any way over the past year?

ACME's finance group and investor relations will continue to track sales and revenue results worldwide on a monthly basis, as well as changes in stock price. However, over this same two-year period, these results will also be incorporated into the monthly company portfolio redesign project measurement reports.

Product research and development teams will closely monitor the approved future design standards and guidelines for new products as developed for this project. Any element of the new standards and guidelines that becomes difficult to incorporate will be brought to the attention of the strategic design manager immediately. The design brief project team shall continue to meet on a monthly basis with representatives of senior management to discuss and evaluate these monthly reports.

The total time frame to complete this project to the point of implementation is thirty-four and one half weeks (8.6 months). The total budget for this project is $303,600. Implementation worldwide will cost $1,000,000.

Note: There you have it—a complete road map for the project. This section is also a useful project tracking device, a formal agreement between all parties, an educational tool for your nondesign partners, and a terrific way to demonstrate design is a complex, strategic process.

This example was based on a major activity for any company—the complete redesign of its entire company portfolio. Therefore, the cost undoubtedly seems very high to you. It probably would seem high to senior management as well! But, by breaking the activities and costs down by phases, it becomes difficult to disagree with the numbers. What activity could senior management possibly eliminate for a project with such high stakes—the ultimate survival of the company in its category? It might also be interesting for you to think about what this project would cost if the price of design labor had been factored in. This is another reason I strongly advocate that in-house corporate design groups be centrally funded. The cost of each employee for the year remains the same to the company whether they do one or two major projects or one hundred smaller ones. Of course, smaller projects than the one in this example would be described very differently. Again, that is why I keep saying each design brief will be unique. It must be developed for a particular project for a particular company. I chose this kind of example because I wanted to include a wide variety of issues that I had discussed earlier.

I'd also like to point out the efficiencies a design group can offer if you routinely assemble competitive materials and build a company portfolio matrix of your own. Ultimately, it will save you a great deal of time, and senior management will be very impressed with your group.

I suspect many readers will argue that there is an awful lot of testing called for in this design brief. They would tell me that their management wouldn't allow all that time and money for testing. For reasons I have already covered earlier in this book, testing is what will allow a corporation, and its design group (whether internal or external), to know whether they are on the right track or not. In my career, when I encountered resistance to all the testing I was recommending, I would simply ask senior management how much time it would take, and how much more would it cost, if we implemented a new design and the target audience reacted negatively. Would we have the time and money to do it all over again? Usually they had to agree, especially on high-visibility projects such as the one in this example. If you are asked to do a project that is considerably lower in risk, you would probably not have the time and money to do such extensive testing. In those cases, I would simply do my own informal testing, as described earlier. I would personally visit a dozen or so customers in the company of a salesperson making routine sales calls and get some reactions from customers by myself. No matter what, I would want some target audience input.

Research Data

The primary missing research data for this project includes an R&D forecast for the types of new products under development (or planned at this time), the approximate timing of their introduction, and the market analysis and target audience demographics and description for these new products. This information will be critical to the development of the design standards, guidelines, principles, and strategies for future new products. The design team will not be able to develop a comprehensive plan without this data.

(Name) from R&D and (name) from the market research group will be accountable to provide this data to the strategic design manager no later than (date). Additionally, the finance group will agree to do a cost-benefit analysis for this entire project based on the costs budgeted in this design brief. This report will be prepared by (name) and presented to the design brief team no later than four weeks following the start of work on this project. This report will be made available to (name of final approver) by this same date.

Note: There is really not a great deal of missing research data in this excerpt. As mentioned in chapter 3, there are many times when no data is missing; in those cases, this section may be deleted.

This example of a design brief did not include much about those standards and guidelines for new products mentioned in the project overview and background section. This is because critical research data is missing. It doesn't mean the project cannot begin. It simply means that about a third of the way through the various phases this data will become necessary to complete the project. People have been identified to supply the data, and a date has been established. This is okay for now. If the data is not supplied in a timely manner, there is a written record in the design brief that it was required. This eliminates that old excuse, "If you had only told me sooner you would need this information..." It's a matter of record now.

Finally, the cost-benefit analysis is mentioned. Prior to having an approved design brief, costs were only estimated. More than likely, the costs were underestimated! Now that the design brief team knows how much the project will really cost, it is wise to ensure that the investment is worthwhile. Additionally, this financial analysis will be of enormous help to you in preparing your approval presentation and in the measurement process after the new design solution has been implemented. Alerting the final approver now is politically correct. You don't want that person to faint when you go in for final approval and he asks, "How much did this cost?" If there is going to be problem, better to get it out in the open now, before you have gone very far.

Appendix

The appendix will be updated weekly as new material is completed. Contents include:

- Report of visual audit of ACME Company's portfolio, as well as of Brands X, Y, and Z.
- Results of phase 3 global concept testing.
- Results of phase 4 global concept testing.
- Executive summaries of external testing agency findings for global tests of recommended final design solution.
- Complete copy of final approval presentation.
- Complete copies of project implementation plans written and approved by various corporate functions, as described in phase 7.
- Project cost-benefit analysis from corporate finance group.

- Copy of R&D new product development plans.
- Copy of market research new product market analysis and audience demographics.
- Measurement metrics questionnaires, plus monthly executive summary reports.
- PDF files of all major concepts initially explored by the design group.
- Competitive materials and data.

Note: As mentioned before, the appendix becomes a collection of "stuff" that really doesn't fit anywhere else. The whole design brief, including all of the material in the appendix, will become valuable archival material for future projects. Creating great design briefs actually becomes easier and faster with each one you develop. Very often, materials from one project will be absolutely essential to another project. Why keep reinventing the wheel? Archive your design briefs.

Chapter 13
Anticipating and Overcoming Obstacles

As a result of teaching my approach to design briefs and to moving the design function from a service group to a core, strategic business competency, I have learned that designers and design managers are intimidated by what they see as insurmountable obstacles. Most people tell me that they would love to get to the point of being an equal partner, accountable, a co-owner, and a key strategic resource, but in their company culture it will never happen! There are too many obstacles. Well, sure, there will be obstacles you will encounter. There are obstacles in almost everything we do in life. But instead of wringing our hands and saying it can never work, let's see if we can address those obstacles head-on.

Unanticipated obstacles are the single most important reason why plans fail. Every designer or design manager who wants to create a plan for improvement for his or her function should place significant emphasis on visualizing obstacles before they arise and make strategic plans for dealing with them.

Two Kinds of Obstacles

Conventional wisdom describes two broad categories of obstacles that can get in the way of progress: personal obstacles, and environmental/technical obstacles.

Personal Obstacles

Some personal obstacles include:

- Fear of failing
- Fear of authority figures
- Fear of accountability for decision making
- Low tolerance of, or for, change
- Risk avoidance
- Lack of specific business knowledge or training
- Lack of experience
- Lack of constructive feedback and sense of support
- Lack of personal drive or ambition
- Inability to speak articulately in front of groups
- Procrastination
- Confused priorities
- Reacting—"fighting fires!"

Pretty grim list, don't you think? The fact is that everyone has some of these lacks, fears, and traits to a greater or lesser extent. It's very important to honestly recognize them in yourself, because it is possible to change or to deal with these obstacles, neutralize them, avoid them, or go around them.

But personal obstacles are difficult because overcoming them often requires you to change habitual and comfortable ways of behaving. Also, many design managers and designers never really face up to their personal quirks. Many entertain a number of misconceptions about how they are really perceived by various constituencies.

If you recall my exercise wherein I ask each participant in my seminar to make a list of how he perceives himself, and then a second list of how he knows he is perceived by others, there is always a disconnect. Human beings tend to see themselves under a different lens than others do. Therefore, it is critical to think long and hard about your personal obstacles, and then to seek feedback from others about how you come across (even though I know this is risky).

When I was with the Gillette Company, the company hired a consultant to help group managers with just this kind of dilemma. The consultant developed a form that was circulated to all of our direct report employees, as well as to the individuals we came in contact with on a daily basis outside of our particular department. The form asked these people to answer many questions about each manager, including an area for narrative, general comments. When these forms were completed, the consultant analyzed the collective results and then met with each group manager on a one-on-one basis to go over the results.

The identity of who had made each comment was kept in strict confidence by the consultant. Neither the results of his analysis nor the source of any specific comment was ever revealed to the company's senior management; therefore, none of this became part of anyone's employee record. The purpose was solely to provide group managers with accurate feedback about how they were being perceived by their staffs and other peers. The process was very revealing, to say the least.

At first, I was a bit frightened by the concept. I think everyone was frightened. But the consultant was a professional with this process, and he quickly eliminated our fears. I learned that some of my behaviors and practices could be improved. It wasn't that I was some kind of miserable failure, just that I was doing some things that were getting in the way of my becoming the kind of manager I really wanted to be. The consultant offered very positive and supportive suggestions of ways in which I could overcome some of these barriers and obstacles to my success. The key would be to develop a personal plan for improvement. I really must say, this process was one of the most helpful exercises in my career. It made me pause and reconsider some of my day-to-day practices. It made me aware of places I could improve. It was also the basis for my strong belief in making personal plans—which I will address in chapter 14 in more detail.

I have suggested trying this kind of exercise to many design managers, and they have also responded favorably to the effort. A relatively simple and inexpensive way to do this is to develop your own set of questions, distribute them to your staffs and peers, and ask them to respond—anonymously, of course. This may be the quickest way to determine what your particular personal obstacles to success really are, and then to do something about these obstacles.

Environmental Obstacles

On the other hand, environmental/technical obstacles are those blocks to success that you seem to have little or no control over. They come from others in the organization, from company culture, or even from the world outside the company. The list could be very long, but the most common environmental/technical obstacles I have encountered include:

- Lack of time
- Lack of budget
- Lack of staff support
- Lack of equipment
- Business conditions/climate
- Competitive pressure or disadvantage
- Lack of adequate physical space in which to do your work
- Other people's personal obstacles

These environmental/technical obstacles, combined with your own personal obstacles, often make dreaming of any kind of improvement seem impossible.

Dealing with Obstacles

The best way to deal with an obstacle, whether personal or environmental/technical, is to face the obstacle head-on. Sit down and make a list of all of these apparent barriers to your success. Describe your personal obstacles in detail, and then list your environmental/ technical obstacles. For each item on your list, ask yourself, What will happen if the obstacle remains? Who are the people, other resources, time issues, and pressures involved with this obstacle? Can this obstacle be eliminated? How? Can this obstacle be neutralized? How? Can I change or modify my plan or it's timing to get around this obstacle? How? How serious is this obstacle—really? How much time and effort is it worth to overcome this obstacle? What new behavior would help overcome this obstacle? What help could I get from others? How do I get that help? How long will it take to overcome this obstacle?

Listing your obstacles, then asking yourself these questions, will, at a minimum, help you focus on finding solutions rather than just saying, "Ain't it awful?" The process should also help you realize exactly what is getting in the way of your success.

There are just a few things that can happen. You could eliminate the obstacle, neutralize it, go around it, or, live with it! I will be the first to admit sometimes you simply have to learn to live with it. For example, I worked with a company that had experienced a devastating fire. Most of its headquarters burned to the ground. Temporary office space was found for employees in various other locations around the city while the headquarters were rebuilt. The design group lost all of its equipment and files. Work had to begin all over again on projects currently in progress. Management said that the deadlines could not be changed. This was certainly a technical obstacle that the design group was forced to live with for a time. There wasn't really much that could be done except to face the problem, work day and night, and try to get back on track.

There were a few members of the design staff who wanted to mount a major effort to delay the due dates of projects underway. The manager—quite wisely—realized that this would not be a good plan. Everyone else in the company was facing the same dilemma and was working diligently to get back on schedule. For the design group's members to complain that their needs were unique and that they therefore needed special treatment would not make them appear like business partners. It would only reinforce the idea that they were just a service group. It was very stressful for almost a year. This is an example of an obstacle that the design group simply had to live with.

On the other hand, I know of another situation in which the design group simply did not have adequate space to effectively accommodate their workload. Repeated pleas by the design manager for more space were denied. The cost per square foot was prohibitive—at least, that is what the finance people said. The design manager changed his tack and went forward with a plan for space that emphasized *revenue generation* per square foot. The design manager was able to demonstrate that a portion of the increases in sales and market chares were directly linked to the *results* of design activity. By using this argument, the design manager was able to effectively relate revenue increases to the facilities required by the design function to generate those revenues. They got their extra space.

For personal obstacles, it will often be necessary to seek help from sources outside of the company. Most human resource departments are aware of a variety of professional development programs, which can help people improve their personal skills, behavior patterns, and abilities. I have seen hundreds of cases where design managers were able to improve their presentation skills or negotiating skills, or overcome shyness and reluctance to be proactive, by utilizing external resources to help them with these issues.

The important thing is to identify all of your real, imagined, or potential obstacles, analyze them, and develop a sound plan to deal with them. Things will never get better until *you* take some positive steps to make them better.

Chapter 14
Creating a Plan for Moving Ahead

Assuming you are not completely satisfied with the status quo and assuming you are serious about elevating the design function in your organization to a position of core, strategic business partnership, then you will have to develop a comprehensive plan to achieve your goals. Simply wanting it or thinking about it will never work. You will need to carefully and strategically develop an action plan to get you to your objective.

You might even need to develop two plans: a personal plan for improvement for yourself, and a group plan for your design staff. The techniques are really the same for both activities. Get yourself a notebook and start designing a written plan.

Step One

The very first thing to do is to determine your real, added value to the company. (Review chapter 7, as well as the comments from various design managers in chapter 9). This should be both your personal, added value, and the value your design group adds to the business. Write your value statement(s) down in the notebook.

In chapter 7, I presented a variety of techniques to get you started. At this point in developing an actual written plan, try adding a few more exercises to those previously mentioned techniques. Make a list of accomplishments and failures—both your personal ones and the ones for the group. The key to learning from this exercise is to be completely honest with yourself. The discipline of writing down and reviewing your past triumphs and mistakes will help you pinpoint areas in which you need to focus or improve your management style and your group's practice. Be careful to ensure that the accomplishments on your list are meaningful to the business. Simply saying, "I/We have never missed a deadline" is not enough. People who run businesses expect, as a matter of course, that you will always be on time, on budget, and on objective. That's why they pay you in the first place. It's not really an *accomplishment*, it's a given. Rather, accomplishments have to do with activities that have made things work more effectively. Accomplishments are those things you have done that have genuinely advanced the strategic business objectives of the enterprise. Accomplishments are things that can be *measured* in one way or another.

The mistakes are also important to recognize. If something went wrong, why did it go wrong? What could you have done differently? Why didn't you?

A couple of years ago, I attended the DMI European Conference in Amsterdam. Among the many excellent presentations was one by an officer from the United States Army. Yes, the Army! This officer was a training specialist, and he described an activity that I believe should be used by design groups everywhere. At the end of each training exercise (as well as actual combat situations), all of the participants would attend a debriefing meeting. He explained that this activity had to occur immediately after the event in order for details to be fresh in every soldier's mind. They would discuss what went well and what didn't go so well. They would explore reasons for both. Why did a particular maneuver work to their advantage? What could they have done differently to make the maneuver even more successful? What unanticipated events arose? How well did they meet the challenge of these events? What mistakes were made? Why?

I believe that this technique could be very valuable for design groups. Immediately upon completion (and approval) of a major design project, assemble the design team and have just this kind of discussion. Be sure to include your co-owner/partner for the design brief in this meeting. Take notes and make these notes part of your ongoing action plan for improvement. Pay particular attention to those areas that did not work as well for you as you had hoped. Then, develop a plan in your notebook to ensure that your next project will address these issues adequately.

After going through this process, you should be able to clearly identify areas that will need some concentrated work, as well as the areas of strength that you need to use in articulating your added value as a core business competency.

The PAR Formula

The PAR formula has been around for decades. I really don't recall where I first learned about it, but I do know that I have used it for more than twenty years to help me sort out my various action plans for improvement. It's really very simple.

"P" stands for a *Problem* you faced that required unique action on your part. "A" is for the *Action* you took to solve the problem. "R" is for the *Results* you obtained.

Look back over the years you have been a designer or design manager. You can probably recall examples of actions or events of which you can be particularly proud—as well as some that didn't work out very well. The ones for which you are proud are your achievements. What is important is that these achievements summarize your current skills, your ability to solve problems, and your ability to take positive action. Some examples that may help you get started:

- You improved workflow processes and developed a successful implementation plan.
- You found meaningful ways to shorten or improve the design process cycle.
- You recognized a serious problem and took positive action to fix it.
- You produced design solutions that increased market share, competitive advantage, the bottom line, and so forth.

This exercise will be very meaningful to your plan for improvement. Again, by writing these things down in your notebook, you will be able to begin understanding which actions you have taken in the past that produced positive results and which actions often led to negative results. This same process relates to the debriefing meeting I just mentioned. What problems arose, what action did you take when the problem surfaced, and what were the results or outcomes of this action? If you don't write these things down and take a hard look at the lists, you will undoubtedly never really focus on the areas in which you need to improve.

Play on your strengths, and develop a list of weaknesses that need to be addressed. Now, using a calendar, set dates—real dates—and a list of actions you will take by those dates to eliminate, or overcome, your weaknesses. The key for all of the activities I will describe is to set *dates* for actions. If you don't set realistic dates, your plan will never work. It's too easy to say, "I really have to get to that someday." You'll never do it. Trust me!

I will confess that one of my personal obstacles is that I tend to procrastinate. It is remarkably easy for me to say to myself, "I'll get to that next week." And then next week, I will find another very rational reason to put the activity off a little longer. It is best never to say to people like me, "I'll need this some time in the spring." You won't get it until midnight the first day of summer! The only way I have been able to overcome this personal obstacle is to be sure I set exact dates for completion or delivery of an action item. For me, an exact due date on my calendar forces me to plan my time effectively. I feel pretty certain that many of you are the same way.

A Master Plan Needs to Be Specific

Returning again to chapter 7, do the same kind of thing for each of the sections of the model. Get hold of an organization chart and determine the role design plays in each function of the company. Set dates for contacting people in those functions and for offering to come by and have a chat with them about their design issues. Plan in advance what kinds of help you are able to offer. Write all of this down in your notebook! Always relate design to *their* needs and the needs of the company. Remember what John Tyson would say in a meeting: "I'm here to *invest* in your future." Never, ever, go into these kinds of meetings with a list of *your* problems or issues. "They" don't really care about your problems.

By the same token, as you develop function-by-function lists of design's uses and design needs, begin to develop a list of the individuals in each of those functions with whom you need to develop mutually valuable relationships. How will you meet them? A cold call? Should you get someone to introduce you? Who will that person be? As always, set real due dates for these activities—and then meet those due dates.

Getting to the "Right" People

It is critical to develop an internal network of people in your organization who can help you get visibility, credibility, and trust. But how do you find these people and make meaningful contact with them? The following suggestions will help you get started:

- Use the organizational chart to get a list of names.
- Do some research to find out which of them are the actual stakeholders in design issues.
- Determine whether they have had any previous experience with your design function. Was it positive or negative? Why?
- Consider what design issues they will most likely be facing in the short term—and the long term.
- Find out who their mentors, friends, allies, and detractors are.
- Finally, develop a plan to meet with them.

Before your first meeting with these individuals, prepare questions that demonstrate your knowledge of both the company's business issues and its specific business issues. Ask many questions. Don't try to "sell" design or the design function. Rather, focus on how you can effectively partner with your colleague and contribute to his or her success. After you meet with each person for the first time, always suggest a follow-up meeting at which you can present some ideas of how design can help solve some of his or her business problems, and specifically, how your design group can work with him or her to solve these problems. It's also a good idea to invite him or her to visit your turf. Schedule an exact date and time for a next meeting. Don't ever simply say, "I'll get back to you." Rather, you should be saying, "I'll meet with you on (date/time) to go over a definitive plan with you." It's also a good idea to follow-up these meetings with a memo, e-mail, report, or some other written document. Above all, *nurture* these new relationships.

Obstacle Planning

Work through the list of obstacles to success you created earlier. Develop concrete plans (again, with specific dates) for overcoming these obstacles in the most effective way possible. Involve your entire staff in creating all of these plans. It really should be a group effort.

Action Plan Formatting

There are as many formats for "action plans" as there are management gurus who devise them. All of them, in my mind, are equally effective—if they work for you. The format of your personal plan is just that, personal. If it works for you, it's a good format. The important criteria to include are the specific actions you must take to reach your goals. Prioritize this list and include completion dates for each item. Note the specific steps you will need to take to achieve each goal, and devise a way to measure progress. Above all, stick to your plan.

A few typical goals of such plans include:

• Getting the company to value you and the design function
• Becoming the recognized expert in design issues
• Becoming a key contributor to the business, not the "art person"
• Becoming essential to the success of the business
• Becoming a strategic business partner

I have worked with several design groups that actually did take the time to create a plan for "resetting" the design function in their companies but then carefully filed the plan away when the workload got particularly heavy. Please don't do this. The development of a plan, and then adhering to that plan, is the only way to achieve your goals for the design function.

It is the responsibility of the design function's manager to take the leadership role in this process. Many years ago, when I first managed a small corporate design group, I believed I could not only manage the group but also do some design projects myself. At the time, it seemed to be the best of both worlds. Unfortunately, as I began to realize what it really meant to be a design manager, I also had to face the reality that I would have no time to do design work myself. It was a tough decision. I would venture to say that all of the really great, successful design managers I have known over the years faced the same realization. A design manager must have the time to manage and lead. This will most likely mean you won't have time to do design projects yourself. It's worth giving some thought to this. If you want design to be a center for excellence, a valued and trusted partner in the corporation, and a strategic contributor to the overall success of the business, then the design function needs, and deserves, full-time leadership. It is a major commitment.

Chapter 15
Lessons from the Trenches

As a way of summarizing the key elements included in this book, I would like to offer a few final thoughts derived from my many years of managing corporate design groups, consulting with a large number of global corporations, networking and talking with many peer design mangers, teaching seminars, presenting workshops for in-house corporate design groups, and lecturing for a number of design associations. Lessons from the trenches, if you will.

As I mentioned at the outset, the professional training in design I received, primarily at the University of Connecticut and UCLA, prepared me well to embark on a career as a designer. However, this training gave me very little insight into the ways of the great corporate world.

I spent the first five years after graduate school teaching design at a small private college. I thoroughly enjoyed my initial (short) teaching career. Teaching offered me an opportunity to settle down and rethink many of the things I had learned in my own college career.

It also provided me with the opportunity to travel in the summers. I spent a great deal of time in Europe going to museums, meeting and talking with European designers, and visiting a few European design schools. All in all, that five-year investment in the teaching profession ultimately helped me immensely.

However, I reached a point where I believed that it was time to enter the corporate world and start "doing real design." To say that I immediately felt "thrown to the wolves" is an understatement! It didn't take very long to realize that what I believed I had to offer wasn't really valued that much by nondesign business managers. I quickly joined the ranks of designers who whined constantly about not having enough time, not having enough budget, and being generally abused and taken for granted as an "artist." I was not a happy camper.

Fortunately, I had a few mentors during my career who offered me some valuable guidance. It was these people who told me I needed to find a way to learn more about *business*. I was enrolled in an executive development program at the University of Michigan. It was a one-year program that probably changed my life.

In the article on design management by Earl Powell in chapter 9, Earl describes how hard he lobbied for funds for his design group staff to attend various professional development programs. Earl realized, as many of us have, that just being a graduate of a design school will never be enough. Designers in the corporate arena need to develop their managerial, leadership, and business skills—the stuff we didn't get in design school.

What has come to be known as "professional development" in the corporate world takes on several meanings, depending on your particular areas of responsibility. For some managers and executives, it means pursuing an MBA at an accredited business school. For others, it is participation in extended executive development programs, such as the one I attended at the University of Michigan, which are offered by various colleges and universities worldwide as part of their extension programs. For many managers, it is attendance at various seminars with titles like "Training the Trainer," The Art of Negotiation," "Conducting Effective Performance Reviews," or "Accounting for Nonfinancial Managers." All of these types of programs have their merits—as well as their drawbacks.

Many managers find participation in a full-time MBA program just too strenuous when added to the already heavy demands of their jobs and their families. College or university extension executive development programs are typically easier to accommodate, since they typically are designed as a series of one-week residency programs over a course of a year or more. They do tend to be pricey and are often scheduled at times when it is inconvenient to be out of the office for a week at a time.

The one- to two-day seminars seem to be the most popular, both for price and for minimizing time spent away from the office. For all of these options, the trick is to decide which programs are best for a design manager whose aim is to advance in the ranks of management. For others, their companies make the decision easier for them by mandating areas the managers need to improve in at the time of their annual performance review. Exploration of these programs should become an integral part of your personal plan. Your plan, if done the way I suggested, should reveal the priority areas that you need to focus on very clearly. So, one very important lesson from the trenches is to continually explore and participate in a variety of professional development programs.

DMI Seminars

Unfortunately, except for the various seminars offered by the Design Management Institute, there are very few professional development opportunities designed *specifically* for the design profession. That is why I was asked to develop a few seminars for DMI to help fill this void.

The first seminar was given the title "Managing the Corporate Design Department" and was designed specifically for managers who were struggling with the need to elevate design as a core competency in their organizations—rather than just being a service group. Later, I developed a new workshop, "Making the In-house Design Function a Strategic Competency." This was offered exclusively to in-house, corporate design functions, involved with graphic design, package design, or industrial design. Each workshop is tailored to the requesting group's specific and unique needs. The results of these workshops have been impressive for me. In-house design functions *can* re-invent themselves and become respected in a corporate environment.

It took about six months to design the seminar, and the process involved a number of people. I consulted with professional course developers, industrial psychologists, experienced (and successful) design managers, and nondesign managers in a number of corporations. This process was very revealing for me—especially the comments from nondesign managers. The most important findings were that design is not well understood at all (and therefore not highly valued by nondesign management) and that designers and design managers have generally had very little formal training in business. It was also very clear that the most successful design mangers in the industry *did* know how to clearly articulate the value of design and *did* know the role of design in business. These basic findings became the core of the seminar content. For the most part, designers and design managers do not seem to be very good at clear business communications.

This research helped to further crystallize my own thinking about the future of the design profession. Designers and design managers absolutely must learn to speak a new language—the language of business. I also realized how critical a tool this design brief business is, not only for executing design projects but, perhaps even more importantly, for changing the perception of the design function as a whole in any enterprise. Lesson from the trenches number 2: improve your *business* communication skills, and use the design brief process as a tool to communicate the strategic, added value of design.

The design brief process I have described offers nearly all of the powerful opportunities really necessary to persuade nondesign business partners that design is a core business competency that plays a major role in the success—or failure—of any business.

Using the Model as a Guideline for Change

The research also led me to developing the model I outlined in chapter 7. I have been using this model for more than a decade. Although a few people have had some problems getting it to work for them, the vast majority of people who have implemented it report that within a year or so, perception of design as a valued partner had increased dramatically in their organization. It really does work. But don't kid yourself—it won't work overnight. Meaningful change always takes an investment of time. If you are not prepared to invest the time and effort necessary to effect positive and meaningful change, nothing will ever improve. You will continue to be the overworked, under-appreciated service provider.

I strongly suggest that you take the various elements of the model, one by one, to your staff meetings. You only need to set aside twenty minutes or so at each weekly meeting to discuss the various topics. Involve everyone in your design group in the discussions of each element. Try the exercises, then develop a group plan of action. Lesson number 3: develop a comprehensive action plan—and follow it. And, lesson number 4: always involve your entire design group in developing plans for improvement of the function. Don't try to do it all alone.

Most of us have had to fumble around for years in the trenches, trying to make sense out of apparent madness. Now is the time to stop fumbling around and make some changes. Use this design brief process as a vehicle to help you make those changes quickly and efficiently.

Finally, I'd like to offer you several of my general "precepts" that I discovered in the trenches over the years. I have touched on most of these in more detail in this book:

- *Involve others in the work of the design function.* This doesn't mean designing by committee, but rather, valuing business input from others. Know your key stakeholders and *talk* to them.
- *Be careful of the terms you use when describing design activities.* You are not the "art service bureau." You don't have "clients" or "customers," you have business partners. You don't work "for" people, you work "with" people, who are your associates.
- *Get your nose into everything that has to do with the business of your company.* Read the business press to learn more about your industry. Attend major industry trade shows. Ride along with salespeople as they contact customers. Attend major sales meetings, and talk to attendees about what they are seeing in the marketplace. Visit every functional group in the company. Learn about their activities and their business issues. Determine what role design plays in each function. Then become an ally, an advisor on design issues for every facet of the business.
- *Understand, then effectively communicate, the added value of design to the success of the business.* Become an ally—a partner—particularly with marketing people. You will be attending to challenges they never even thought about.
- *Take your show on the road.* Leave the design studio and take a tour through your business. Send pertinent design articles to strategic supporters. Write a monthly or quarterly article emphasizing the value of design for your internal employee newspaper or magazine. Think about producing your own "Design Quarterly" for employees. Don't emphasize beauty or cleverness; rather, emphasize business results and benefits of good design.
- *Enlist the support of your CEO—or at least claim you have it!* Do everything possible to ensure that the CEO is aware of your positive business contributions to the company. Invite him or her to visit your studio.

- *Research executives to raise consciousness.* It will make them part of the solution when you ask them about their issues and concerns. When they are part of the solution; they are truly your partners.
- *Create an easy-to-understand design policy statement for your function.* Include strategic objectives in the policy. You will need one for credibility.
- *Get your own budget.* Potential supporters won't come to you if you are going to charge them for the privilege. You must be easy and accessible to partner with—not costly.
- *Involve your staff in every discussion.* They will feel empowered, involved, and more motivated.
- *Invest all the time that is required to achieve your goals.* Over the long term, it will actually save you time in the future.
- *Network with other design professionals outside of your company.* Isolation only leads to loneliness and narrow thinking. Attend design conferences and seminars to meet with your colleagues. Keep in touch with them as you share ideas, strategies, triumphs and failures. Learn from one another.
- *Pursue ongoing professional development opportunities.* Use your human resources group for assistance.
- *Never, ever, forget the target audience.* Know and understand the people you are designing for.
- *Always think strategically.* Become a leader, not a follower. Be proactive.

In conclusion, the single, most critical lesson from the trenches is that in order for design to have credibility and trust in the organization, designers need to learn how to think and communicate in a different way. Designers need to be able to articulate the value of design clearly and simply, in terms that are more about the benefits of design than the design itself. They need to study the business in depth and to determine the roles of all kinds of design activity in that business. They also need to proactively develop partnerships and alliances throughout the organization in order to get the support and trust they so desperately want. Finally, design needs to be a true strategic business partner throughout the organization, working *with* people, not *for* people. It is possible to bring design up out of the "trenches" and onto the organization's main playing field, but it is up to the design profession to make this transition on its own.

About the Author

PETER L. PHILLIPS
Design Management Strategy Consultant

Peter L. Phillips is an internationally recognized expert in developing corporate design management strategies and programs. He has had more than thirty years experience as a senior corporate design manager, a consultant, author, and lecturer. He distinguished himself in the corporate world as Director of Corporate Design for the Gillette Company and as Director of Corporate Identity and Design for Digital Equipment Corporation. In both positions he had global responsibilities for managing strategic design functions.

Mr. Phillips' corporate career has crossed several industries. In addition to his Gillette and Digital Equipment Corporation assignments, he has been a television set designer and producer for Group "W" Westinghouse Broadcasting, Director of Promotional Program

Development and Design for Stanmar Inc., a major East Coast resort developer and operator, and president of his own design management firm.

As a consultant, Peter has developed numerous global design strategy programs for many Fortune 500 companies. He also advises corporations on restructuring, and repositioning, their in-house corporate design groups.

Peter takes a highly pragmatic, business-based approach to all of his assignments, believing that design, and the management of corporate design functions, is a problem-solving discipline rather than a simple aesthetic exercise.

He has been the recipient of numerous awards and honors including the prestigious *Financial World* Gold Trophy for design of the Best Annual Report in the United States, as well as for development of promotions, promotional material design, communications, and for designing and implementing effective brand management systems.

He is also the author of *Principles of Managing the Corporate Design Department*, a section of the anthology *AIGA Professional Practices in Graphic Design* (Allworth Press, 2008), and numerous articles for the *Design Management Journal.*

He has also contributed to the books *Careers by Design* by Roz Goldfarb (Allworth Press, 2001), *Revealing The Corporation*, by John M.T. Balmer and Stephen A. Greyser (Routledge, Taylor & Francis Group, 2003), and *UX Best Practices, Processes, and Techniques: Achieving Impact with User Experience, by Helmut Degen and Xiaowei Yuan* (McGraw-Hill, 2011).

Peter Phillips has been a columnist for both *Graphis* magazine, and *New Design* magazine. The British Design Council has engaged him to create a knowledge cell and video on design briefs for their website: (www.designcouncil.org.uk/briefing)

Phillips has developed case studies on brand identity for DMI and the Harvard Business School that are being distributed by the Harvard Business School. He was a member of the former Design Management Advisory Panel for the University of Westminster (London, England) Business School. He also served on the Advisory Board and was an adjunct professor in design management for the Suffolk University Executive MBA Program in Innovation and Design Management. Phillips has served as a member and secretary of the board of directors of the Design Management Institute (DMI). In addition Phillips is an Honorary Director/Advisor of the Hong Kong International Jewelry Designer Association.

He founded the DMI Professional Development Program and develops and conducts workshops for design management professionals worldwide. His workshops are offered as in-house, on-site, training for corporations. Along with Professor Emeritus Stephen A. Greyser of the Harvard Business School, he is the codeveloper and copresenter of a Senior Executive Workshop program entitled, "Strategies for Developing, Maintaining, and Sustaining a Powerful Brand."

He is a frequent guest speaker for a wide variety of organizations in the United States, Europe, and Asia. Topics include: Creating the Perfect Design Brief, Developing and Implementing Strategic Global Design Programs, Managing the Corporate Design Department, and Selling Strategic Design Up the Corporate Ladder.

Phillips earned a Master of Arts Degree from the School of Fine Arts, University of California at Los Angeles, and a Bachelor of Fine Arts Degree at the University of Connecticut. He has also completed the curriculum requirements for a PhD in Fine Arts at UCLA and has completed post-graduate studies at the University of Colorado, and the University of Michigan, School of Management.

Selected Bibliography

Books

American Institute of Graphic Arts. *AIGA Professional Practices in Graphic Design*, edited by Tad Crawford. New York: Allworth Press, 1998

Balmer, John M.T., and Stephen A. Greyser. *Revealing the Corporation*. London: Routledge, 2003

Borja de Mozota, Brigitte. *Design Management: Using Design to Build Brand Value and Corporate Innovation*. New York: Allworth Press, 2004

Chajet, Clive. *Image By Design From Corporate Vision to Business Reality*. New York: McGraw-Hill, 1997

Cohen, Alan R. and David L. Bradford. *Influence Without Authority*. New York: John Wiley & Sons, Inc., 1990

Made in the USA
Coppell, TX
24 August 2024

36346195R00142